Heal Me, O LORD

The Christian's handbook to personal wholeness through healing prayer

Calvin R Tadema

D0950535

Heal Me, O LORD: The Christian's handbook to personal wholeness through healing prayer.

© 2015 by Calvin Tadema

Published by Two Worlds Press, a division of Two Worlds Media of Brush Prairie, WA (www.twoworldsmedia.com).

ISBN-13: 978-1505821215

ISBN-10: 1505821215

Acknowledgements

If you cannot express yourself on any subject, struggle until you can. If you do not, someone will be the poorer all the days of his life. Struggle to re-express some truth of God to yourself, and God will use that expression to someone else. Go through the winepress of God where the grapes are crushed. You must struggle to get expression experimentally, then there will come a time when that expression will become the very wine of strengthening to someone else; but if you say lazily - "I am not going to struggle to express this thing for myself, I will borrow what I say," the expression will not only be of no use to you, but of no use to anyone. Try to state to yourself what you feel implicitly to be God's truth, and you give God a chance to pass it on to someone else through you.

Always make a practice of provoking your own mind to think out what it accepts easily. Our position is not ours until we make it ours by suffering. The author who benefits you most is not the one who tells you something you did not know before, but the one who gives expression to the truth that has been dumbly struggling in you for utterance.[1]

These words from *My Utmost for His Highest* have been a reminder, encouragement, prod, and command to me through which I have completed this book. It has been a struggle to express myself because words are so inadequate when it comes to the supernatural ways of God. Yet, in the words of my friend, Jim Morud, "writing exacteth the mind."

I want to thank my wife, Julie Tadema, for her constant support and encouragement as prayer partner, ministry partner, and life partner. My best friend, Dan Friesen, for reading and re-reading the manuscript to "exact my mind" a little bit more. My co-laborer and friend, Dan Mayhew, for preparing the work for publishing. My parents, Rits and Pearl Tadema, for an incredible spiritual inheritance.

The board of directors for Master's Mind Ministry has been a great support: they are Ron and Ruth Hartford, Charlie and Karen Pudwill, Dan and Jody Mayhew, and Dan and Linda Friesen. In addition, I acknowledge our Prayer Shield which is made up of prayer warriors from all over the globe. I could feel the power of the Spirit unleashed by their worship and intercession.

Finally, I want to thank the people that helped me articulate the concepts in this book. Thank you to my friends that share coffee times, workshops, and seminars to ask hard questions, especially you who press for deeper meaning and clearer understanding. Thank you, also, to those who have met with me and my wife for prayer. God teaches us many things as He speaks truth to you.

Praise the Lord!

Contents

Introduction   1

Chapter One: Heal me, O LORD   5

   Definition of Healing   7

   Greek vs. Hebrew Worldview   10

   Shalom   17

Chapter Two: Save Me   23

   The Purpose of Pain   24

   Redeemed by God   26

   The Role of Faith   31

Chapter Three: Prayer for Healing   35

   Anatomy of a Prayer Appointment   37

   Confident Prayer   43

   Listening Prayer   50

   The Power of God   58

Chapter Four: The Human Construct   61

   Body   62

   Spirit   63

   Soul   64

   Three Realms   66

Chapter Five: Spiritual Realm   71

   Authority   71

   Legal Ground   74

   Curses, Oaths and Vows   78

Chapter Six: Emotional Realm   83

You Are What You Believe   83

Inner Healing   88

Mind Renewal   89

Interrogate Beliefs   90

Persistence of Identity   93

Chapter Seven: Physical Realm   99

Signs and Wonders   101

The Ways of the Lord   104

Your Highest Authority   107

Chapter Eight: Complete Healing   111

Reconciled to God   112

Reconciled to Self   115

Reconciled to Others   119

Chapter Nine: Interceding for Others   121

Sharing Hope   121

Loving Through   123

Sharing Truth   124

Free Indeed   125

Cautions and Practical Matters   126

Chapter Ten: Prayer Strategies   133

Addiction   135

Trauma   139

Anxiety   141

Physical Healing   142

Inner Healing   143

Rejection & Abandonment   145

Betrayal   146

Chapter Eleven: You are My Praise   149

Redeemed Story   150

A Suitable Thank Offering   151
Resources   155
    About the Author   155
    Other Titles   155
    Speaking and Teaching   156
Endnotes   157

Introduction

"... for I am the LORD, your Healer." - Exodus 15:26

I was fourteen or fifteen years old when Laverne came to visit our home in Fountain Valley, California. She was loud and round, walked with two canes, and kept her legs tightly wrapped in ace bandages. I remember that her legs stuck straight out when she sat because she had to keep her feet elevated. I thought she was strange, so my goal was to give her space.

Laverne struggled with many health issues and asked my mom to pray for her. Though her faith was small, she travelled all the way from Alberta, Canada for the opportunity. Word had gotten out that my mom's prayers were powerful and effective.

By the end of one week, Laverne was a different person. She was still loud and round, but there was no avoiding her ebullient embrace as she bellowed: "Calvin, my boy! Give me a hug!" Her joy was complete as she walked and danced until her face glowed.

She left her canes and ace bandages at our house when she flew home. Her subsequent phone calls and letters reported on the goodness of God and the continuation of physical and emotional healing. She was a testimony to God's power and mercy, and never shied away from declaring His truth. For many years after, and in many houses since, those canes hung on the wall as an Ebenezer[2]. They were a testimony to the woman who left them behind and the God who loved her so deeply.

Many years later I talked with my mom about the spiritual gift of healing. I asked her how she came to know her special anointing for it.

"I've never thought that I have a special anointing" she answered. "To expect God to heal in answer to our prayers is available to all of us as believers. I guess if there is anything special it is that I took God at His word: that we can ask Him for anything according to His will, and He will give us what we request of Him."

This book is about the ministry of healing today for the normal Christian. It does not presume a special anointing or appointment by God. It does not presume a special doctrine, belief system, or enhanced level of faith. It does not presume specialized training or education.

Rather, this book assumes the ministry of healing is performed by the power of God, according to His will, in and through agents of His choosing. All Christians should expect to receive healing, and expect to witness healing in others.

Some of the concepts and ideas we have discovered in our ministry over the past decade help open the way for healing. Each chapter in this book is designed to simplify the message and give the reader confidence to pray fervently and boldly for himself and others.

סלה

My wife and I were deeply involved in our local church in the late 1990's. I volunteered as an elder, taught adult Sunday School, and headed up the Men's Ministry. Julie served as the leader of the Women's Ministry, led Bible Study groups, and mentored young mothers. Soon people sought us out for spiritual guidance, godly advice, and prayer.

Our hearts were moved to compassion for God's children as we listened to their stories and heard of their pains. We wondered how our loving heavenly Father would bring healing to them. We prayed and asked Him for insight and guidance.

A woman struggled with outbursts of anger and a harsh tongue. She was desperate to keep her family, but in her pain she drove her husband and children away. She would try to win them back, promising to change, but before long the ugly cycle would begin again. There is a proverb that describes her inner conflict: "The wisest of women builds her house, but folly with her own hands tears it down.[3]"

"Pray for me!" she insisted. "I want to change but I can't seem to break out of this miserable life. Can God help me? I don't know where else to turn."

Her story was filled with abuse, rejection and abandonment. She didn't choose this life; it started when she was just a little girl. The abusers were supposed to love and care for her, but instead they charged her with being crazy. She wondered if it was true. Sometimes it felt true. She was suffering the consequences of sin committed by others.

Our hearts moved to compassion for this woman. There was no quick biblical bandage to slap over the problem. Every Christian catchphrase, motto, or slogan fell short. The spiritual disciplines, acts of contrition, and efforts at strong self-control had already failed her many times.

One evening my wife prayed: "Lord, can you fix what's wrong in her life?" Then she continued, "Because I just don't feel like lying to her anymore. If You can heal, show me how. But don't expect me to tell her I'll pray if it doesn't really do any good."

That prayer, offered in frustration, opened the way for us to receive information. First a trickle came through books and articles from those that have been ministering in divine healing for years. Soon it became a flood of revelation as we began to recognize the language and witnesses that God has been using to bring healing to His children.

The purpose of this book is to share the things God revealed to us in answer to prayers like this. We do not believe this to be a new revelation, but a general revelation that He has been giving to many people in this generation.

The Lord spoke through Moses to tell His chosen race: "I am your Healer" (Exodus 15:26). In the Hebrew language the word used for healer is *Jehovah-Rapha,* the same for the word physician. It is God's promise to be our doctor.

Jesus encouraged the disciples on the night He was betrayed by telling them He would send the Holy Spirit. Then He gave this incredible promise:

> *"Truly, truly, I say to you, whoever believes in Me will also do the works that I do; and greater works than these will he do, because I am going to the Father.* - John 14:12

Let me paraphrase this promise to emphasize the truth it contains. If you believe in Jesus, and that He came from and returned to the Father, then you are authorized and responsible to do the works that He did, and even greater works. Proclaim the Kingdom, cast out all demons, cure diseases, and heal sicknesses[4].

May you be blessed as you read these pages, and may the Holy Spirit quicken the truth in you so you are equipped for the work of ministry and to attain to the measure of the stature of the fullness of Christ.[5]

Several illustrations, testimonies, and stories of healing are shared in this book. Each is used to help make a point or express a thought. The names used are not the real names of people that have received help through Master's Mind Ministry. Although many have given permission for us to share their story, I chose to use fictional names. There are similarities in the countless stories we have heard, and common circumstances behind them. For that reason, you may recognize yourself or an acquaintance in these examples by association

Chapter One:
Heal me, O LORD

Heal me, O LORD, and I shall be healed; save me, and I shall be saved, for You are my praise. - Jeremiah 17:14

What a profound statement of faith! Take a moment to ponder this verse. Meditate on it. Repeat it silently and aloud until you have soaked it into your inner being. It is a key that unlocks the simple truth about God's will for you.

"Heal me, O LORD."

This is a simple request by which you may ask to be mended or made whole. It acknowledges the need for change and implies childlike faith in receiving His response. The prayer is directed to the LORD, a title that represents His absolute sovereignty. It reminds us that God has all power and authority, and He can use it any way He wants. Healing you is well within the scope of His power.

"... and I shall be healed."

This is a simple profession of faith. It declares that the LORD is willing and able to heal, and the healing is completed by His will.

I believe a lot more people would experience healing if they just prayed this simple prayer.

The parents of a six year old girl were making arrangements to take her back to the Emergency Room. She had been sick for two days and the fever was returning with a vengeance. Even though nothing conclusive was discovered the night before, it seemed like the only thing to do.

"Mommy, I don't want to go back there. Would you pray for me instead? Jesus can make me better."

A desperate mother was moved to prayer by her daughter's childlike faith: "Heal her, dear Jesus. Make her better."

The fever broke fifteen minutes later and the young girl fell asleep peacefully.

A simple request made with childlike faith moved the heart of God to intervene in the spiritual, emotional and physical realms to demonstrate His great love for His child.

Praise the Lord!

I had opportunity to pray with a man that struggled with alcohol for over forty years. His life was a mess because of his drinking, and he wanted to be rescued from the addiction. He drank out of loneliness and rejection. He came from a family of alcoholics and began drinking before he dropped out of high school. He had hit bottom.

He confessed as sin that he rejected God's ways and chose to self-medicate with alcohol instead. He forgave his family members, including his ex-wife, for rejecting him. A sense of peace came over him as the truth of forgiveness entered his heart.

"Would you like me to pray for God to heal you from alcohol?" I asked.

He had already told me that in the last twenty years the longest stretch he had been able to "quit" was for four or five days. His doctor had cautioned against quitting cold turkey for fear of stroke or heart attack, though he did recommend that he taper off. It was a hard decision for him to make. I had to press him for an answer three or four times, while addressing his objections along the way.

"Okay, you can ask God to heal me," he agreed reluctantly.

I took a deep breath and prayed: "Lord, he is willing for You to heal him from alcohol addiction. Please heal him now, and set him free. Amen."

He was healed. He did not have another drink, not even a sip. He did not have a stroke, heart attack, or any other symptoms of withdrawal. His co-workers were amazed and his boss was proud of him for what he had done. They asked him how he had been able to finally quit drinking.

"God healed me!" he said. "That's the only explanation I have. I've never been able to do it myself, but God healed me."

Praise the Lord!

Can it be this simple?

Can we expect answers like this every time we pray?

Can we declare "When You heal me, I am truly healed, O LORD?"

What does it mean to be healed?

Definition of Healing

> *Behold, I will bring to it health and healing, and I will heal them and reveal to them abundance of prosperity and security.* - *Jeremiah 33:6*

The context of this verse is the prophecy of Jeremiah regarding the fall of Jerusalem to the Chaldeans. God had given the word to him, thereby predicting the destruction and captivity that was about to take place. Then God shared this secret with Jeremiah about His plans for after the time of captivity.

I like this verse because it uses the words health, healing, and heal. It provides a framework from which we can understand God's promise to Jerusalem. When God says "I will bring to it ..." the object for Jeremiah is the city of Jerusalem, but prophecies have multiple meanings. In that way it also refers to His chosen race, and by extension the New Jerusalem. According to 1 Peter 2:9-10, we are that chosen people and this promise applies to us.

"I will bring to [My people] health ..." The word "health" used here has the connotation of closing a wound or restoring wholeness. A priority of first aid is to stop the bleeding, to close the wound, so that a victim may live. A subsequent priority is to restore health in the body to function according to its design.

"I will bring to [My people] health and healing." The word "healing" in a Biblical context means a cure, deliverance, or medicine. It carries the flavor of ongoing improvement or treatment toward wholeness. In other words, healing means to bring curative influences and conditions to the person. It can also mean to bring deliverance from conditions leading to disease, decay and death.

"... and I will heal them ..." The word "heal" means to cure or to doctor. It suggests the action of being a physician or the pursuit of doctoring.

In Exodus 15:26 we read: "for I am the LORD, your Healer." God had just promised His people that if they would listen and obey Him they would not experience any of the diseases that He put on the Egyptians. In other words, as long as you listen to and obey God, He will be your Doctor. The doctor takes on responsibility for His patient, but the patient must do as instructed. Since the LORD is completely trustworthy as a Doctor, the known outcome of His doctoring is complete restoration and wholeness.

Returning to Jeremiah 17:14, if we substitute doctor for both occurrences of the word "heal," it is paraphrased this way: "Doctor me, O LORD, and I will be Doctored." Again, the outcome is as reliable as the Physician.

The end of Jeremiah 33:6 says: "... and reveal to them abundance of prosperity and security." This is not an additional clause in the promise, but a continuation of the assertion. This little phrase is translated differently in various versions of the Bible. For instance, the King James Version renders it "peace and truth," while the New International Version uses "peace and security."

One of the reasons for different translations is that this Hebrew text uses the word *shalom*. In that culture and language this little word is a thesaurus all by itself. It has many variations of meaning depending on the context in which it is used, but all aspects of it are good. So all the terms are applicable: prosperity, security, peace, and truth.

As I contemplated the meaning of the words health, healing and heal, it dawned on me that peace and security are the outcome, results, or byproduct of being healed. In other words, they are the symptoms of healing. We see this over and over in the prayer room.

Imagine being plagued by a panic attack so severe you fight for breath and every cell in your body is filled with tension because you are paralyzed by panic; unable to choose between fight or flight.

You pray this simple prayer: "Heal me, O LORD." Immediately the panic subsides as peace wells up inside you and comfort washes over you. In a moment the tension has been replaced with warmth and contentment, as if Jesus were right inside you. It is *shalom.* You have been healed.

God heals using natural and supernatural means. As I write this I want to emphasize that God is <u>always</u> supernatural, so all His ways are supernatural. It is man's way of understanding that distinguishes between natural versus supernatural, but there is value in exploring this distinction.

I remember a conversation with a man who was learning about healing. He had done much of his research through the writings and teachings of well-known healers, and he was trying to put it into practice. He was disappointed with the results when he asked God to heal his strep throat.

"I prayed aloud and believed with all my heart that God would heal my throat," he shared. "But He didn't. I finally gave up and took some medicine."

"So, what happened?" I asked.

"Well, I got better," he confessed. "The antibiotics kicked in, I got some rest, and my throat cleared up in a few days. But I wanted God to heal me!"

He was disappointed because he was "believing for" a supernatural healing. In the ensuing conversation he realized that he felt like God had ignored him and let nature take its course. Instead of a miraculous healing, he had a very normal and predictable return to health.

I reminded him that God instructed Moses to place a tree in the bitter water to make it sweet (Exodus 15:26), Elisha put some flour in the poisonous stew to make it edible (2 Kings 4:38-41), and there are many other examples where God healed things through the natural realm. We should let God be the Doctor, and not presume to instruct Him in how to go about it.

Naaman was such a man, wanting to dictate to God how he should be healed. But when he came into agreement with God's will and way, he was cleansed from leprosy, which was considered an incurable disease.[6]

Shouldn't we come into agreement with the will of God regarding healing? If it is God's will to heal someone by natural design and order, let them agree with His will and be healed. When it is God's will to override the natural laws to heal someone, then let them agree with His supernatural will and be healed.

A big part of the problem is that we are self-referential in our definition of healing. We have a personal idea of what we want it to mean, and we place some expectations on how it should be achieved. To truly understand healing, we must learn to see things from God's perspective.

Greek vs. Hebrew Worldview

My friend John Kozy and I have been meeting regularly for several years to discuss health, healing, and what it means to be healed. John is ideally suited for these conversations because he is a doctor of chiropractic, a Christ-follower, and a seeker of truth.

During one discussion I shared that some of the people my wife and I prayed for had been changed so dramatically, it was as if they had become new people. On the other hand, others slipped back into their old ways shortly after being healed. Still others had prayed earnestly but not seen any positive results from the prayer time.

John was intrigued and related that he had experienced similar outcomes with the patients in his clinic. We began to share concepts and brainstorm ideas in a search for truth about healing. His area of ministry is primarily in the physical realm. As an intercessor, I brought experience in the spiritual and emotional realms to our talks.

We observed that the human body is regenerative. It was designed to repair itself and return to proper function, in a process biologists call homeostasis. Examples of this are the body fighting off illness or disease, or repairing a broken bone or torn skin. The body is designed to restore itself to proper functioning. Counteracting this is a degenerative influence on the body by the process we call aging.

So we do not lose heart. Though our outer self is wasting away, our inner self is being renewed day by day. - 2 *Corinthians 4:16*

How does one establish a standard or definition of health with these opposing forces at work in one body? Before we can answer that question, we must consider our frame of reference, the cultural lens through which we see the world.

Most westerners have adopted a worldview based on Greek philosophy. In this perspective science and logic are core values, and truth is established by physical laws and properties. For instance, a person is a living body that operates like a machine made up of various parts. That a person has some non-physical awareness beyond himself is largely unexplained in this frame of reference.

The Greek worldview is primarily physical and rational.

The Hebrew worldview is more like eastern philosophy. In this perspective relationship is a core value, and truth is established through spiritual laws and properties. In other words, a person is a spiritual being that is contained in a physical body. This view is more concerned about the whole, rather than individual parts.

The Hebrew worldview is primarily spiritual and relational.

To illustrate the differences, consider Michelangelo's Statue of David as a masterpiece of Renaissance sculpture. This is a Greek representation of perfection and beauty: a strong young man, perhaps in his mid-twenties, with no defect in form or function. It is a standard of superior physical strength and ability.

Now contrast that image with this prophecy about Jesus:

> *For He grew up before Him like a young plant, and like a root out of dry ground; He had no form or majesty that we should look at Him, and no beauty that we should desire Him. - Isaiah 53:2*

The only One who was truly perfect did not fit the Renaissance model. He had no beauty or ideal form, yet He was considered righteous by God. The Scripture says:

> *Therefore ... consider Jesus, the apostle and high priest of our confession, who was faithful to Him who appointed Him, just as Moses also was faithful in all God's house. For Jesus has been counted worthy of more glory than Moses ... [because] Christ is faithful over God's house as a Son. - Hebrews 3:1-6*

This indicates that perfection, or glory, is measured by faithfulness to God and His house. In other words, perfection is "being in complete harmony or agreement with God and His character." The connotation of perfection is "being complete, mature, whole, or properly established." This is the perfection modeled by Jesus.

The clash between eastern and western perspectives is nothing new. In the Garden of Eden, Adam and Eve were deceived into leaving their harmonious relationship with God, and instead were convinced of their ability to rationalize good and evil. The original sin was that of choosing to depend on reason rather than relationship.

At the time of Jesus' ministry, the Pharisees fell into the same sin by choosing to be governed by the law rather than love. Their law was fixed and rational, and subject to their control by interpretation. Love is relational, can be unpredictable and unexpected, and is not easily subjected to one's control.

Fifteen hundred years later two major movements transformed Europe: the Renaissance promoted physical sciences while the Reformation returned to the spiritual. The schism is still in evidence today. A scientific (Greek) worldview all but ignores the spiritual and elevates the importance of the physical: things seen, felt, weighed, measured, and compared. The relational (Hebrew) worldview assigns spiritual and unseen influences very broadly. How much of today's polarization between science and religion, church and state, is rooted in the divergence of these two worldviews?

It is this western worldview that exacerbates the health enigma. When one measures health solely in the physical realm, and then compares that assessment to a phantom standard, there will always be a gap. Furthermore, as the body ages the trend line of natural health declines because of the sin induced, God ordained process of dying. Healing, in a physical sense, becomes impossible.

Using the statue of David as an example, you can see that the idea of "perfect" is a phantom standard. It cannot be achieved. The statue implies soundness of mind and emotions, as well as physical beauty. No one can look and be like David, at least, not for very long. As Paul said: "Our outer self is wasting away."

For a poignant illustration of this conundrum do a quick internet search for actors who have tried to gain or regain their ideal image of health. Many experienced horrific results. The plastic surgeons are willing to do the procedure, but time is ticking away. The physical body is subject to death, and the standard for perfect health is on a downward slope.

The problem with this western understanding of health and healing is that it leads to dissatisfaction. As a person strives for improvement from their "less than perfect" state, they can never be content. First they become dissatisfied with themselves, but ultimately they are dissatisfied with God.

What then is perfect? Does God offer to make us perfect?

Consider a health checkup in a typical western hospital or clinic and you will discover a scientific frame of reference to measure and compare every possible detail in the physical realm. The implied question is: "Am I healthy, doctor?"

In the assessment phase you will be measured for blood pressure, heart rate, weight, strength, reflexes, mobility, and more. The unseen realm is overlooked, except that the less visible indices of health are measured through X-rays, scans, and graphs. The conclusion is delivered with authority:

"Good news. Everything has tested normal. Your vital statistics are all within a range we consider acceptable, for a person your age."

This does not mean you are perfect; theoretical improvements are possible. This means you are healthy. That is to say, you should be satisfied with your condition because it is unreasonable to expect measured improvement.

If we say that healed, perfect, and truth are synonyms for the sake of this discussion, then you can see how the western worldview derives truth by calculation and comparison. Truth is relative. It is discovered through reason and defended with statistics.

For example, the standard for perfect visual acuity is 20/20. In this sense I mean "perfectly acceptable" not theoretically ideal. This value is calculated by how clearly a person sees at twenty feet, compared to what the average person sees from the same distance. Although renowned test pilot Chuck Yeager had a better than average visual acuity rated at 20/10, a person does not usually ask for healing from 20/20 vision. They are satisfied with normal vision even though it is possible to see twice as well.

Two inconsistencies of the western view arise, as it relates to healing. First, some conditions are accepted as "normal" because they represent the average experience of others. People accept "average" and do not request or expect healing beyond the norm. Second, some conditions are considered defects because they do not fit the ideal. People reject "average," yearning for the phantom standard. In either case, the unseen and unmeasurable problems are ignored.

סלה

In the Hebrew worldview truth is not relative. Truth is a Person, the person of God. In this context there is room for absolute truth outside of the physical realm. It is discovered by insight, a benefit of relationship, rather than calculation.

Adam and Eve were perfect in the Garden of Eden because of their relationship with God. God declared that it was good. He does not have a good, better and best option, but everything He declares to be good is perfect. Adam and Eve were physically perfect because every aspect of their created being was suited for the harmonious relationship they had with God, each other, and the world.

Sin threw them out of relationship with God, as evidenced by their shame and hiding strategies after they sinned. God promised to restore the relationship and redeem them from the consequences of their sin.

For the wages of sin is death, but the free gift of God is eternal life in Christ Jesus our Lord. - Romans 6:23

Remember that God created man as an immortal spiritual being in a physical body. The result of sin is death. The free gift of God is eternal life.

Spiritual immortality comes through physical mortality.

God's ultimate definition of healed is to have eternal life in Christ Jesus which means spiritual immortality in a resurrected body. The physical realm aspects so integral to the Greek view will pass away, and new aspects that have true value in the Hebrew view will be eternal.

God does not define healed as the opposite of dead. Quite to the contrary, He defines complete and total healing as the outcome of having passed from death to life.

Does God heal people with cancer, restoring them to a pre-cancerous state? Absolutely. I can testify because my wife was healed from lymphoma in 2007. I have seen many healed from cancer through our ministry and the prayers of others.

But we must keep the main thing the main thing. God's plan is not to give us immortality in our physical bodies. He kept Adam and Eve from eating from the Tree of Life to avoid this. He shortened human lifespan at the time of the Flood to hasten the complete healing process. Lazarus and others that had been raised from the dead would have to go through the dying process again, though they probably had no fear of it.

> *And this is eternal life, that they know You the only true God, and Jesus Christ whom You have sent. - John 17:3*

God's definition of complete healing is relational and eternal.

Meanwhile, God is healing in the here and now as well as the hereafter. It is a process in the present and ongoing tense, and encompasses the physical, emotional and spiritual realms. He is the Master Planner, setting the sequence and timing as it pleases His will, yet never overriding our free will.

> *And we all, with unveiled face, beholding the glory of the Lord, are being transformed into the same image from one degree of glory to another. For this comes from the Lord who is the Spirit. - 2 Corinthians 3:18*

There is no question of God desiring to heal. He paid the ultimate price for the right to heal. The Lord, the Son of God, sacrificed everything to pay the penalty for the sin that separates the Father's adopted sons and daughters from Him.

We can say with all confidence that we are being transformed into the glory of the Lord[7] from one degree of glory to another[8]. Sometimes His plan seems to be slow, but that is because of His mercy and patience. He knows the right timing and never stops the process of healing us. Sometimes His plan seems to stop, but that is because the person He wants to heal is unwilling to let Him.

This book is written to encourage you to come into agreement with the Lord, your Healer and accept all that He has to give you.

Shalom

Peace I leave with you; My peace I give to you. Not as the world gives do I give to you. Let not your hearts be troubled, neither let them be afraid. - John 14:27

Josh came for prayer to deal with some of his behavioral issues. We asked the Holy Spirit to guide our time, and reveal the source of these actions. Josh felt an emotional distress that exactly matched the way he feels whenever he is alone. It is almost unbearable to him, and he acts out in several different ways if his family has to be gone for any length of time.

We asked the Holy Spirit to guide him to the source of that feeling. He immediately recalled a night when his parents had left him home alone and there was a severe thunderstorm. He was fourteen years old and embarrassed about "being a baby," but the fear was real. As we examined that emotion, he came to realize that it was a fear of death, and more specifically a fear of spiritual death.

I prayed that God would show him the truth and heal him from the fear.

"Oh!" he said shortly. "Jesus was with me during that storm. It's OK, I can feel His presence, and everything is peaceful and calm."

"Check into the fear of spiritual death," I asked him, "and tell me if that is still there."

"No, it's gone," he replied. "Right where I felt that fear gripping me before, now it's warm there." He was pointing toward his chest as he answered me. "The fear is completely gone, and everything is fine."

Josh was healed in that moment from the fear of being alone, the fear of spiritual death, and all the emotions and behaviors that had been part of his life because of that fear. In place of that fear he had *shalom.*

Remember that *shalom* is a "symptom" of healing. Here are some words that are included in the definition of *shalom:* well, happy, friendly, health, prosperity, peace, favor, friendship, greeting, blessing, rest, welfare, wholly, and contentment.

Jesus performed many miracles and healings that are recorded in the Gospels. In the healing of the paralytic at the Pool of Bethesda, he tells the man to get up, pick up his mat, and walk. After thirty-eight years of not being able to get up, carry, or walk, this action proved he was healed. The "symptoms" of healing in the physical realm are evident through our five senses.

When a person experiences forgiveness a great weight is taken off his shoulders, a darkness is lifted off his soul, a warmth fills his heart, or a sense of contentment rises up within him. These are "symptoms" of healing in the unseen realm.

One of the observations made by my friend John Kozy is that people pursue healing when they perceive a problem, such as a disease, sickness, or dysfunction. Sadly, many of them stop pursuing health when they are asymptomatic.

For instance, a person with a chronic pain in her knee becomes dissatisfied with her health. In this culture, she begins to seek medical advice and help because of the pain. If the pain subsides, then the symptom of disorder is gone. She no longer looks for the source of the problem, unless the pain resumes. A pain killer or other form of symptom treatment does not address the root issue. It only removes the incentive for true healing.

On the other hand, healing may be taking place in her body that goes undetected because of the presence of pain. So pain itself is not the most reliable symptom of health, or lack of it.

True *shalom*, on the other hand, is an accurate measure of our relationship with God, and our true health. Even when there is disorder in our circumstances or body, it is possible to have peace.

> *So we do not lose heart. Though our outer self is wasting away, our inner self is being renewed day by day. For this light momentary affliction is preparing for us an eternal weight of glory beyond all comparison, as we look not to the things that are seen but to the things that are unseen. For the things that are seen are transient, but the things that are unseen are eternal.* - 2 Corinthians 4:16-18

God invites us to eternal life. It is His will to bring us completely to that state. When we agree with His will, our healing is certain to begin immediately and last forever. Paul provides another example of this truth later in the same letter to the Corinthians.

> *Three times I pleaded with the Lord about this, that it should leave me. But He said to me, "My grace is sufficient for you, for My power is made perfect in weakness." Therefore I will boast all the more gladly of my weaknesses, so that the power of Christ may rest upon me. For the sake of Christ, then, I am content with weaknesses, insults, hardships, persecutions, and calamities. For when I am weak, then I am strong.* - 2 Corinthians 12:8-10

Paul is not suggesting that weaknesses, insults, hardships, persecutions, and calamities are to be sought. Quite the contrary! He pleaded three times that the Lord take his infirmity away. God was more interested in the relationship than Paul's temporary health. Paul became content with the condition when he knew it served God's purpose.

19

Nevertheless, do not rejoice in this, that the spirits are subject to you, but rejoice that your names are written in heaven." - Luke 10:20

Jesus emphasized this point as well. The disciples were amazed that even unclean spirits were subject to them. In that day sickness and disease was synonymous with demonic interference. Jesus kept the main thing the main thing: "your names are written in heaven." In other words, it is worthy to rejoice that demons, sickness and disease are all subject to the authority of Jesus, but do not lose sight of the real goal: eternal life.

I taught a lesson on healing at a large Christian church a few years ago, and after the session a woman came to ask a question. She had been suffering from chronic pain for many years, and had pled for healing throughout that time. Her husband quickly confirmed that they had been to several healing services, as well as receiving prayer from many ministers.

"I wonder, should I just learn to accept this condition or should I keep asking in faith for God to heal me?" she asked

"Do you want to stop asking?" I replied.

"No, I still want to be healed," she answered. "But it's getting harder to believe."

"Is your pain something that stands in the way of your relationship with Jesus?" I asked. "Do you have any resentment against God or others because of this pain?"

"No, I've really checked my heart about that. I truly believe that I'm in right relationship with God." After a short pause she continued: "and others."

"Has God told you to stop asking?" I pressed.

"No," she answered thoughtfully.

"Then let's ask Him again," I said, and I began to pray for her physical healing. It did not immediately manifest, but when they left it was with a new sense of peace. They agreed to keep asking God for healing, but with contentment that God has a plan and purpose not yet revealed.

While on earth, God gives us the benefits of Sonship, and encourages us to receive all His good gifts. The real definition of healing is *shalom*, and the ultimate *shalom* is to spend eternity with God

Chapter Two:
Save Me

Heal me, O LORD, and I shall be healed; save me, and I shall be saved, for You are my praise. - Jeremiah 17:14

God had a purpose for Adam and Eve. He told them to be fruitful, multiply, fill the earth, and subdue it. They were to be stewards over the physical realm as representatives of God. They had everything they needed to fulfill this purpose: authority over the earth, free will to choose how to exercise that authority, and direct communication with God for guidance.

This was their divine design. Their identities were a perfect blend of self and love. On the one hand each was a uniquely created person, able to reflect the image of God with self-expression. On the other hand each was so filled with His love that they were other-centered rather than self-centered.

The original sin, eating the fruit from the Tree of Knowledge of Good and Evil, was the first self-centered act. Adam and Eve chose to think of themselves more highly than they ought to think and divorced the perfect love of God. They accepted responsibility for knowing good and evil, and it cost them their direct communication with the Holy Spirit.

Ever since that sin every human being is born with an identity crisis. Designed to be an object of love that loves unconditionally, the self turns that affection inward. Instead of loving God and our fellow man, we squander that love on self-protection, self-awareness, and self-centeredness.

Thankfully, God did not abandon mankind to this fate, but immediately made a way to save, rescue, and restore him. God's unconditional love persisted and He began reconciling the world to Himself through Christ.

That is why we can claim this promise of Jeremiah: *Save me, and I shall be saved.*

The Purpose of Pain

> *And the LORD God commanded the man, saying, "You may surely eat of every tree of the garden, but of the tree of the knowledge of good and evil you shall not eat, for in the day that you eat of it you shall surely die." - Genesis 2:16-17*

What did God mean when He said "in the day you eat of it you shall surely die?" The immediate consequences of sin are pain and toil, and ultimate death is to return to the dust[9]. This description helps us understand God's warning to mean "in that day you shall surely *begin* to die."

Humans are generally pain intolerant, especially of pain without a purpose. We will go to great lengths to avoid it or make it stop. Some, at the first hint of pain, go to medical professionals for answers. They want someone to fix it, numb it, or cut it off; to do whatever it takes to make the pain go away.

Pain is a very powerful attention-getter. Unfortunately, many people are satisfied with symptom relief, and once the pain has subsided or become tolerable, they go on their way. They act like the man in James 1:23-24 that intently evaluates himself, but then goes away and at once forgets what he discovered.

Pain with a purpose is treated differently. It is amazing how much pain the human body will tolerate when the person understands its purpose. For example, a woman giving birth has extreme pain, but she no longer remembers the anguish when she sees her baby (John 16:21). The pain she endured is offset by the value of the purpose.

When our identity is different than what God created us to be there is conflict. Where that conflict exists there is pain. The purpose of pain is to point to the source of the conflict.

We use the term "identity in Christ" to describe our divine design, because that is the way God sees us through the lens of redemption and reconciliation. We are reconciled from our active identity (who we are being) to our identity in Christ as we die to our self and live for Him.

Jehovah-Rapha is the compound name from Exodus 15:26 where God says: "I am the Lord, your Healer." In other words, He is our great physician. When He told Adam and Eve that they would surely begin to die, He left them time to be rescued by Him.

The scheme of the devil is to hold people in bondage through fear of death (Hebrews 2:14-15). He also uses the fear of pain, which I call the fear of the dying process. Then he tempts people to believe that God is the source of the pain, either because He caused it or because He has not eliminated it. The person is held captive by that fear, and God gets the blame.

But I love the way God reverses the enemy's schemes to fulfill His ways. Imagine that this Great Physician is asking you: "Where does it hurt?" The answer to this question points to the source of the problem.

Remember, when conflict exists between who you are being and who you were designed to be, that is where there is pain.

Let me illustrate with an example. Charlton described his pain as a sleep disorder. He would wake up in the middle of the night and not be able to get back to sleep. I prayed a simple prayer asking the Lord to reveal the source of this pain.

"It's anxiety about my business. I obsess over decisions I have to make, and ones I've already made," he answered.

I prayed, "Lord, please reveal to Charlton what's behind this anxiety."

"I haven't thought of this in years," he said. He went on to describe being teased by his older brother, and how it made him feel like a failure. Now, twenty-five years later, he was still trying to prove himself.

"Lord, Charlton believed that he was a failure, and in some ways it still feels true to him today. Would you show him his true identity?"

His eyes filled with tears, and he said, "God doesn't see me as a failure. He loves me just as I am."

Charlton accepted his true identity, asked Jesus to forgive him for choosing to be anxious, and was healed of his sleep disorder.

Notice that in this example the pain of insomnia pointed to the sin of anxiety. The anxiety came from the conflict between Charlton's true identity in which he is acceptable to God and his active identity in which he was living as a failure. When he reconciled the differences, the conflict was resolved and the pain went away.

Redeemed by God

> ... In Christ God was reconciling the world to Himself, not counting their trespasses against them ... - 2 Corinthians 5:19

When we cry "Save me, and I shall be saved" it means so much more than merely escaping eternal damnation. Salvation does not begin when we die and return to the dust, but when we die to self-centeredness and return to our identity in Christ.

In English translations of the New Testament there is a distinction between "healed" and "saved" that does not exist in the original text. The Greek word *sozo* means to save, deliver, protect, heal, preserve, do well, or be made whole. Translators use the context to decide which English word to use. For instance, if the reference seems to be speaking of the spiritual realm they use words like "save, saving, or saved." If the context is more in the physical realm it is rendered "heal, healing, or healed."

I point this out because our western worldview tends to separate the realms, and this exaggerates the distinction. If we merge the realms it offers a more accurate sense of the good news as demonstrated by this popular verse.

> *For God did not send His Son into the world to condemn the world, but in order that the world might be* [**saved / healed**] *through Him. - John 3:17*

We see here that it is God's will that the world be redeemed from the penalty of sin and instead be saved, healed, and restored according to His divine design. The word *sozo* is translated in some instances as "made whole" to capture this sense of being integrated (brought back together) rather than dis-integrated. In other words, through the forgiveness of sin we are completely reconciled.

A great example of reconciliation is the old fashioned exercise of balancing a check register. The account holder kept track of deposits and withdrawals to the checking account by recording all transactions as accurately as possible. At the end of the month he would compare his balance against the balance reported by the bank on an account statement. If there was a discrepancy, each transaction was reviewed to find out where the difference was made. Either the bank (unlikely) or the account holder (likely) had made a mistake. The methodical process of comparing, discovering errors, and making adjustments is called reconciling.

God has given the Holy Spirit to convict the world of sin[10]. In a way, the Spirit acts like the account statement by which we become aware of our errors. We are reconciled when we adjust our mind, will and emotions to reflect the truth.

Forgiveness is what closes the gap between who I am being (my active identity) and who God created me to be (my divine design). Jesus has paid the price for that gap, and we are reconciled the moment we accept His forgiveness.

Accepting forgiveness is the essence of being saved, and is no less important for being healed.

Here are the steps for being forgiven:

1. **Conviction** - *be sensitive to the Holy Spirit to know right from wrong.*

2. **Confess** - *take a complete accounting of the sin.*

3. **Ask for Mercy** - *surrender your rights and be humble.*

4. **Receive** - *accept forgiveness as a gift.*

5. **Repent** - *have a renewed mind.*

6. **Reconcile** - *restored relationship is now possible.*

Charlton was not surprised to learn that anxiety was the cause of his insomnia, but he had never considered it to be a sin. He thought anxiety was a normal emotion for everyone. He tried to control it, but accepted it as part of life. He had been this way all his life and believed the worry-chip came factory installed.

I assured him that emotions are neither good nor bad, but are an outcome of what we experience and believe. It is not sin to experience an emotion. When we ask for forgiveness, we do not ask to be forgiven for an event, experience or emotion, but for an offense against God.

Sin is defined as missing the mark; to make an error; to reject a way of God, especially by breaking His commandments. It is an offense against God.

I pointed out to Charlton: "Jesus commands 'Do not be anxious.' Yet you choose to worry. God promises to care for you and protect you, but you ignore Him. When you rely on yourself, you are telling God that you don't trust Him or love Him. The fact that you feel anxious is an outcome of your choice. It is the pain that points to the conflict. The real sin is that you turn your back on God and reject His overture of love."

The Spirit testified to Charlton's spirit, and he understood his sin. He confessed it sincerely, and asked for mercy.

If we confess our sins, He is faithful and just to forgive us our sins and to cleanse us from all unrighteousness. - 1 John 1:9

Charlton described a huge weight being lifted off his chest as he prayed. There was no doubt in his mind that God had heard his plea, forgiven his sin, and cleansed him from all unrighteousness.

Months later I checked in with Charlton to see how he was doing. The insomnia had been healed instantly, and when he was tempted to worry it reminded him to trust God instead.

Praise the Lord!

סלה

Forgiving releases the one who forgives. The unforgiving person becomes a debt collector of the one that has caused the offense. Releasing that person from debt frees the one who does the forgiving.

The Hebrew word pronounced *chesed* captures one of God's most enduring character qualities. It means loving-kindness, everlasting love, and tender mercy. We are created in God's image so our divine design reflects this part of God's nature. Being a debt collector is the opposite of loving-kindness.

For if you forgive others their trespasses, your heavenly Father will also forgive you, but if you do not forgive others their trespasses, neither will your Father forgive your trespasses. - Matthew 6:14-15

This Biblical principle is spoken to encourage us to forgive, not to delineate punishment when we fail to do so. It is God's way of describing being like Him. There is spiritual freedom in forgiving others, just as there is freedom in being forgiven.

Here are the steps for forgiving others:

1. **Take an accounting** - *attempting to forget is not the same as forgiving. Consider what the person owes you (offense).*

2. ***Acknowledge the debt*** - *do not minimize or rationalize it, but consider what it has cost you. Anger is a normal emotional response to acknowledging debt.*

3. ***Accept it*** - *realize that the person does not have the means to repay; past, present or future.*

4. ***Find compassion*** - *consider the person rather than the offense.*

5. ***Release*** *all rights to the debt.*

6. ***Reconcile*** - *restored relationship is now possible.*

Alison came for prayer because of a painful and debilitating autoimmune disease. The Spirit revealed that it started soon after she discovered her husband's infidelity. His sin made her feel angry and rejected. She believed that she was unlovable.

She resisted when asked to forgive him. She felt like she was suffering the consequences of his sin, and that did not seem fair. After some thought, she chose to forgive him and walked through the steps outlined above.

She confessed his offenses to the Lord in prayer, outlining them in detail. Then she stated to the Lord that she released her husband from each of those offenses. As the impact of that began to settle on her, she described a sense of peace and calm welling up from inside.

Her bitterness toward her husband was replaced by the peace of God that surpasses all understanding.[11] She felt her physical strength increase over the next few weeks, and the flare-ups of her ailment subsided. A few months later she reported that her physical healing was complete.

Praise the Lord!

The Role of Faith

And He said to her, "Daughter, your faith has made you well; go in peace, and be healed of your disease." - Mark 5:34

It takes the same faith to be saved as it does to be healed. In the incident of the woman being healed by touching His robe, Jesus told her that her faith had saved her. When He said "go in peace" it means that she had been given the gift of *shalom* in all its fullness. Then He told her to be healed of her disease as well. She was made whole spiritually (saved), physically (healed), and emotionally (peace), all because of her faith in Jesus.

It is important to recognize that the object of faith provides the power of faith.

For instance, supernatural results happen when the object of your faith is God, a supernatural being. Faith is to know and agree that He is, and that He loves. We put our trust in Him, and nothing else.

On the other hand, there is some power in positive thinking. We are created in God's image, after all. Positive thinking is to have faith in faith. It is to believe that control over our environment can be accomplished through that faith. This has been demonstrated consistently over the years. People are made well by a positive mental attitude.

The proponents of this faith in faith, such as new age believers, mystics, and others, have adopted this truth, but they did not create it. God has promoted this way of thinking for thousands of years, as recorded in the Scriptures like Philippians 4:8 and Psalm 138. The power of this kind of faith is based on the character of God being reflected in the person. It has some power.

There are some whose object of faith is an outcome. That means they believe in the manifestation of the healing, and expect their unshakable faith to be the agent through which it happens. Examples of these are faith healers and religious practitioners who claim you can be healed by faith rather than through it.

The problem with this line of thought is that it is limited to the power of wishful thinking. When a person attempts to influence their circumstances in this way it usually leads to frustration and a feeling of shame or guilt.

That is not the way we are saved by faith. We are saved and healed because we believe in the true God and in Jesus Christ whom He sent as a sacrifice for our sin (John 17:3). That is why it is more accurate to say we are saved *by God* through faith.

> *Because, if you confess with your mouth that Jesus is Lord and believe in your heart that God raised Him from the dead, you will be saved. For with the heart one believes and is justified, and with the mouth one confesses and is saved. - Romans 10:9-10*

We activate our faith by confession, which brings our will into agreement with the spiritual, emotional and physical realms. As Paul explains in the verse above, we believe with our heart and confess with our mouth. Speaking our confession aloud calls it into existence in the physical realm.

We also activate our faith with a demonstration through an act of will. In the prayer room, which is any place we are doing prayer ministry, we call this a *faith challenge* because it is a voluntary test of faith that the person takes. For instance, if we agree in prayer for a healing then it is wise to try it out. We encourage someone to test their healing with an action or choice that would have been previously impossible.

I prayed with a man that suffered from stomach ulcers, and then I asked him how he felt. He said his stomach already felt much better. I asked him to think about some of the things in his life that led to stress, and test to see if peace was in its place. He agreed that the thought of stress no longer held power over him, as it had before we prayed. He was building confidence in God as he experienced the healing.

It is not faith to believe in something that is not true. It is deception to believe in something that is not true.

A thing does not become true because we believe in it. We believe in it because it is already true.

A thing does not cease to be true if we stop believing in it. Truth is not an opinion, a solution, or a commonly held belief. Truth is a Person: Jesus Christ (John 14:6).

Faith is believing in the truth because it is true in the prophetic tense. In English we have past tense, present tense, and future tense. These are verb forms that help us communicate in a time-influenced frame of reference. Either something happened, is happening, or will happen.

I use the term "prophetic tense" to describe something that is true (or happening) in the past, present and future tenses all at once. This is part of the Hebrew worldview or relational logic, compared to the Greek worldview that is primarily linear.

Are you saved?

The typical answer from a Greek perspective goes along this line: "Yes, I asked Jesus into my heart when I was a teen. I believe that He answered my request, and I have been saved ever since. Someday I will be welcomed in heaven, and my salvation will be fully realized."

The typical answer from a Hebrew perspective goes along this line: "Yes, I asked Jesus into my heart when I was a teen. It was then that I discovered that God had called me from before I was born, and no one can ever pluck me out of Jesus' hand."

Throughout history we see examples of this "already but not yet" dynamic tension. David was the crowned king of Israel but not the ruling king. He served as a prophetic example of Christ who is the crowned King of the earth, and will be the ruling King.

Therefore, my beloved, as you have always obeyed, so now, not only as in my presence but much more in my absence, **work out your own salvation** *with fear and* *trembling, for it is God who works in you, both to will and to work for his good pleasure. - Philippians 2:12-13*

In these verses, Paul did not teach the Philippians that they were able to earn their salvation; quite the contrary. He declared that God works it out. He stated that they were responsible to agree with Him with such sincerity that it caused fear and trembling. In other words, they had a role to play to accept their salvation.

The answer to the question "Am I saved?" is "Yes, I am saved, being saved, and will always be saved because I am saved in the prophetic tense."

Are you healed?

Only let us hold true to what we have attained. - Philippians 3:16

We walk out our faith in practice every day by living in *shalom* with God, holding on to what we have attained and awaiting complete restoration.

God created us to be in relationship with Him. The sin in the Garden of Eden caused us to break fellowship. He chose to tabernacle among us on earth as a deposit toward the time when we will tabernacle with Him in heaven. That is when we will realize that our *sozo* has always been complete.

Chapter Three:
Prayer for Healing

Let us then with confidence draw near to the throne of grace, that we may receive mercy and find grace to help in time of need. - Hebrews 4:15-16

Jason's pastor suggested that he pray with me about relationship problems that surrounded his life. Although he felt like it was more of a command than suggestion, Jason was very willing to ask God for help. I opened with prayer to welcome God's presence in our meeting and to ask Him to guide our conversation.

One of the volunteers in the children's ministry at church had taken exception with Jason over a minor issue. What began as an opinionated discussion had grown over time into animosity between her family and Jason's. It threatened to disrupt the community of the church. The pastor had wisely recognized a pattern of strained relationships around Jason.

"Lord, would you please reveal to Jason what is going on in him when these relationship stresses happen?" I prayed.

"God didn't say anything, but I feel resentment toward her. I thought I'd forgiven her, but just thinking about it makes me mad," he answered in a few moments.

As we explored the emotion a little deeper, Jason realized it felt like rejection. So we took that feeling to prayer.

"Lord, please show Jason where this feeling of rejection comes from," I prayed.

His eyes filled with tears as he recalled a time when his mother yelled at him. At my request, he filled in some of the details.

"I had probably just turned four, and I remember that I got a little pail and shovel for my birthday. I started digging in the dirt, playing with my shovel, when all of a sudden my mom started to yell at me. I remember that she was standing on the front porch yelling at me for digging in the garden. All the neighbors could hear what she was saying, and that I was a naughty boy."

"And what did you believe to be true about yourself in that moment?" I asked quietly.

"I believed that she was right, that I was a naughty boy, and that's why she didn't want me."

"Let's take this back to prayer," I said. "Lord, thank You for bringing this memory to Jason's mind. Now I ask You to reveal to him what he needs to know about himself and how You saw him at that time."

There was a period of silence, and then Jason sort of chuckled through his tears. I asked him what God had shown him.

"Jesus said: 'That was some pretty good dirt, wasn't it?'"

I smiled at Jesus' gentleness and asked: "What does that mean to you?"

"Jesus knew I was just a little kid. He loved me and didn't think I was being naughty."

"What happened to the feeling of rejection?"

"It's gone," he answered. He didn't say 'What would you expect?' but his tone of voice suggested that to me.

"Would you check in with me on something?" I asked rhetorically. "Thinking about your mom then and now, do you still feel any rejection from her?"

"None," he answered with a boldness that seemed to shock him.

"And, what about the relationship at church, the woman who opposed you, her family, and any others that seemed to take sides in the issue? Do you feel any rejection there?"

He smiled in amazement. "No. None at all."

Then he continued by saying, "I don't think I've ever felt this much peace. For the first time, I believe that I'm OK. I didn't realize that deep down I've always fought against being a naughty boy, but now I know that Jesus didn't ever see me that way."

Jason and I met that day for about an hour. After the inner healing was done, we talked through the steps of forgiving his mother, the woman at church, and some others that he felt had rejected him. We also talked about his new identity, and how to walk in it.

Two years later, his pastor asked me, "Do you remember praying with Jason?" I nodded and he continued, "He's been a completely different man since then. It's amazing."

Praise the Lord!

Anatomy of a Prayer Appointment

I share Jason's story with you to demonstrate how gently and easily Jesus heals those that seek Him. Over the years we have learned some important lessons about how to come into agreement with God on healing, and how to stay in agreement with Him.

Every prayer appointment is different because every person's relationship with Jesus is unique. The following section is offered to give you encouragement and build your faith in asking God to do the supernatural. Whether you are praying for your own healing, or praying with others for theirs, there are some patterns of which you can be aware. It is not a "magic formula" or ritual to be memorized and followed. It is our best glimpse to date of effective intercession.

A Safe Environment

Intercession is an act of love. The person receiving prayer, also known as the recipient, operates at all times according to his or her free will and knows it is a safe environment. Any type of coercion or manipulation would be outside of the bounds of love, and to force anyone to act outside their will is a form of abuse. While the intercessor is free to lead the prayer time and direct the conversation, it must always be with permission.

The first tenet of a safe environment is the assurance of confidentiality. Anything that is discussed or discovered in the prayer appointment belongs entirely to the one receiving prayer. It is their story to tell. The intercessor must maintain complete confidentiality unless given specific permission to share.

The setting contributes to a safe environment or detracts from it. The recipient is the final authority on whether he or she feels safe. One person may feel safest in a public setting where the discussion is covered by the din of conversation; another may only feel safe in complete privacy. Describe your typical prayer setting and ask for acceptance, and be willing to accommodate the other person's needs if possible.

Guard against interruptions. We plan for sixty to ninety minutes for a typical prayer session, and limit outside influences during that time. A closed door and reliance on voice mail for phone calls are good ways to do this.

Our policy is that a man will not pray with a woman, or a woman with a man, unless they are close family relatives. A safe environment allows men and women to pray together in a prayer team setting. This protects both the intercessor and the recipient. Of course, we strongly encourage husbands and wives to pray together at all times.

Opening Prayer

An introductory meeting will often start with conversation about what to expect in a prayer session, background information on the process, and other questions that may be in the mind of the one receiving prayer. It is good to briefly address these topics. This is not a time to hear a person's life story, but the recipient may be anxious to share the reason he or she is seeking prayer.

A session begins with a prayer of agreement, offered aloud by the intercessor. It is an acknowledgement that the purpose of the meeting is for each participant to humble themselves before God in expectation of His truth. It includes a confession that without God's help we can do nothing, so the participants agree to listen and obey. This sets the tone for the meeting, and is a good reminder that our purpose is to take the matter to God in prayer, not to discuss it based on our experiences and opinions.

The closing portion of this prayer is to ask God for specific direction in the time together. Rather than guess what the prayer need is, let God reveal it. Listen to the Holy Spirit for guidance, but allow the recipient to answer according to what God is showing him or her.

Today's Need

Frequently people come to a prayer session with a purpose already in mind. They have a felt need or primary conflict to resolve. Sometimes this is confirmed in the opening prayer, but be prepared for a different item to come up in its place. Expect the Holy Spirit to confirm the direction for prayer.

Do not be surprised or intimidated if the recipient says he is not getting anything like a topic or direction. Even though God has revealed something to him, it is possible that he is unaccustomed to hearing from Him. Return to prayer, asking again that God reveal it to him, and be patient.

"What has come to your mind?"

This is a good open ended question to help them gain confidence in hearing from God. Ask them to consider if their thoughts have changed or if God placed a new thought in their mind during prayer. Ask them if they are experiencing an emotional response, or if they are thinking about a behavior or action they have done.

"Where is the pain?"

When we are being something different than what God created us to be there is conflict, and wherever there is conflict there is pain. Share this context with them so they begin to understand the purpose of their pain and how it points to the place where they need to be reconciled to God. The answer may be physical, emotional or spiritual.

Follow the leading of the Holy Spirit because He has a plan that works best.

For example, I was on a prayer team that interceded for a woman with severe panic attacks. When we asked the Holy Spirit where we should start, the woman's thoughts focused on a tenant in her apartment. She was a little frustrated because she did not want to deal with that issue. She just wanted the panic attacks to go away.

I assured her that God could heal her, but that it was His idea to start with this tenant issue. When I asked if she was willing to go about it God's way, she agreed.

In the next few minutes of prayer, God revealed that her roommate was engaged in occult practices and had introduced a dark spirit into the apartment. When she repented of the relationship and asked God to cleanse her home it completely healed her from panic attacks. God knows how to get to the root of the problem for permanent resolution.

Going Deeper

The goal is to discover the root cause and then ask God for His solution. We call this "praying into the need," which means to focus on the feeling or behavior that presents itself so you can discover the belief that is causing the pain.

If the need is primarily in the spiritual realm it may appear that the recipient has a conflict with God, or with their understanding of who He is. Spiritual issues also show up as broken relationships, especially between family members. If the need is primarily in the emotional realm it may appear as a strong feeling or response to situations. Chronic depression, fear, anxiety, or anger are possible examples. If the need is primarily in the physical realm it may appear as disease, chronic pain, or other type of distress.

Remember that we are comprised of all three realms, each distinct but inseparable. Therefore, a spiritual issue will show up in our emotions and an emotional issue will show up in our physical body. Given time, an issue in any of the three realms, body, soul, and spirit, will manifest in each of the other realms. As you pray, begin with the presenting need and ask God to direct the recipient to the source of that issue.

For example: "God, would You please reveal to John the source of this pain?" Then listen together for God's direction. It may come as a feeling, a thought, or a memory.

Interrogate Beliefs

Do not be conformed to this world, but be transformed by the renewal of your mind, that by testing you may discern what is the will of God, what is good and acceptable and perfect. - Romans 12:2

We are conformed to this world by false beliefs and improper interpretations during our life. We must be transformed by the renewing of our mind. Prayer ministry leads us to hear truth from God so we can replace the wrong thinking that has controlled our identity. We discover this when we take the matter to prayer.

"What did you believe to be true because of that feeling, thought or memory?"

Whether the source of the issue is a recent event or something from long ago, we must press in to interrogate it. What we believe in our heart to be true acts as truth to us. For example, a man that came to believe he was unfruitful lived with that as truth throughout his life. A woman that came to believe she was rejected by her mother lived as a rejected person throughout her life.

Sometimes we have to uncover what we believe with our heart, even though our mind attempts to cover it up. If our heart believes we have been abandoned then all the mental gymnastics to convince ourselves otherwise will be temporary at best. Once the belief has been identified, it is important for the person receiving prayer to confirm it. They may say it in their own words, but they are speaking what they believe to be true in their heart.

The next step is to confess this belief to God in prayer and then ask Him to reveal truth. Sometimes it is best for the intercessor to pray this aloud for the other person. At other times it is much better for the person receiving prayer to be the one to confess it and ask God for truth.

Then be quiet and listen.

Receive Truth

When God reveals the truth to the recipient, it goes right to their heart and replaces the false belief they have been holding. This moment can take great patience for the intercessor, but wait for it. If the Holy Spirit reveals the truth to you before the recipient acknowledges it, hold it in your heart until the recipient confesses it. Then you can use it to confirm the truth.

If necessary, coach the recipient to look for new information in the physical, emotional or spiritual realms. They may hear audible words from God or see a vision or memory. They may have a strong emotional response. They may have an inspiration or message from the Spirit that cannot be put into words. When they know they have heard from God it will replace the false belief they confessed.

It is the role of the intercessor to act as a witness to the spiritual transaction that happens in this prayer. You will bear witness to the event and must be willing to give testimony to the truth.

Mind Renewal

So if the Son sets you free, you will be free indeed. - John 8:36

The truth goes right into the heart of the one that has confessed and is willing to receive it, and it sets them free. The response may be evident in the physical, emotional or spiritual realms. The best word to describe the change is *shalom*, which is God's peace that goes beyond a person's capacity to understand.

"Wow, I feel like a huge weight has just been lifted off of me."

"It feels like God has put a quilt comforter around me, and I just want to stay here."

"It's gone! I can't believe I'm saying it, but it really is gone! I'm pain free."

"Is that it? The fear is gone, but can it be this simple?"

These are few of the exclamations we have heard in the prayer room, often accompanied with tears of joy. Free indeed means the person is totally transformed. It really is that easy (for God), and there is no reason to worry that the healing will go away.

After confirming the healing, it is important to go back into the memory, event, relationship, trauma, or physical pain and check for resolution.

"Think back to that place God showed you as the source of the pain. As you reconsider that now, do you have a sense of peace? Are there any unresolved pieces left?"

Once the recipient has confirmed that they are in a place of peace you can close in a prayer of thanksgiving. If they are comfortable with the idea, ask them to pray first to thank God, and then follow that with a blessing for them.

Ask the recipient to share their story with someone else in the next day or two. This is a practical step that gives God the glory for what has happened. Then make a plan to check in with them again in a few days if you can.

Confident Prayer

Wes had been struggling with alcohol addiction for nearly forty years and had hit bottom, again. I had shared my faith with him that God was the only answer, and that he could be healed.

43

"Are you ready for me to ask God to heal you, now?" I asked. "Because when you're ready, I'll pray and God will heal you. You'll have a brand new identity."

He grappled with his objections and concerns, thoughtfully considering the possibilities. He knew something had to change, and it was beyond his control. He had been warned by a doctor that to quit cold turkey would be difficult and possibly dangerous since his body had been abusing alcohol for so long.

"I'm not sure," he said hesitantly.

"Do you trust that God has your best interests in mind? Do you know that He will take care of you?"

"Yes," he answered. Then after a pause he added, "I'm ready for you to pray."

I prayed and he was healed that very day!

I was able to share that testimony with another friend as a way to encourage his prayer ministry. "That was a bold statement," he said. "You actually told him that God would heal him when you prayed. How could you be so sure that God would do it?"

"This one was easy," I replied. "I was just asking God to do what He already wanted to do! God wanted to heal him, and we just came into agreement with God!"

> *And this is the confidence that we have toward Him, that if we ask anything according to His will He hears us. And if we know that He hears us in whatever we ask, we know that we have the requests that we have asked of Him. - 1 John 5:14-15*

As I interceded for Wes, a scripture came to my mind. It's from the passage in Luke 4 where Jesus quotes Isaiah's prophecy about Himself. It says that He came to proclaim liberty to captives and to set at liberty those who are oppressed. Wes was certainly an oppressed captive to his addiction, and it was interrupting his relationship with the

Lord. I prayed with great confidence because I knew the will of God was to set him free.

"But what if you don't know if it's God's will to heal someone?" my friend asked.

His Declared Will

There are some things that are easy to know. It is always God's will to save. The Scriptures abound with promises, such as "everyone who looks on the Son and believes in Him should have eternal life" (John 6:40). He does not want anyone to perish, but for everyone to come to repentance (2 Peter 3:9). If you call on Him, He will answer you. If you turn to Him, He will save you.

Pray boldly for salvation. Reconciliation is always God's will.

> *If we confess our sins, he is faithful and just to forgive us our sins and to cleanse us from all unrighteousness. - 1 John 1:9*

This is a promise I claim every day. It is always God's will to forgive our sins and cleanse us from all unrighteousness. He does this faithfully when we confess our sins to Him.

This is how I boldly pray with someone that has been convicted of sin by the Holy Spirit. I help them take an account of their offenses against God. Then I ask them to confess them aloud in prayer to Him, while I listen as a witness. After their confession I proclaim their forgiveness by standing on this promise:

> *If we confess our sins, he is faithful and just to forgive us our sins and to cleanse us from all unrighteousness. - 1 John 1:9*

For example, the prayer time with Wes regarding his alcohol addiction followed this pattern. In halting words he prayed: "Lord, it is true that I rejected You and chose to hide from my problems in alcohol. It is true that I believed a lie about who I am and ignored Your truth about who I am. It is true that I have tried to make amends for my sin, but haven't asked You to forgive me. I'm sorry, Lord. Please forgive me."

I quickly added this prayer: "Lord, I stand as witness to this spiritual transaction. I declare that Wes has confessed his sin to You of his own free will, that he does not have the means to make amends, and that he has humbly asked You to forgive those sins. I proclaim by Your promise that because he has confessed, You are faithful to forgive and cleanse him from all unrighteousness. I proclaim his forgiveness to be complete in Your name. Amen."

At the conclusion of the prayer, I asked Wes how he felt now that his sins were forgiven. He described a great weight being lifted off of him, and a sense of wellbeing coming over him. He was describing *shalom*, the symptom of being saved and healed.

Pray boldly for forgiveness. Reconciliation is always God's will.

His Perfect Will

Do not be conformed to this world, but be transformed by the renewal of your mind, that by testing you may discern what is the will of God, what is good and acceptable and perfect. - Romans 12:2

We know God's will by reading about it in the Bible and hearing it through His inspired word. For these big things we only need to know about God, but remember that James writes in his epistle even the demons believe (about) God, and shudder in fear.[12] We must know God as a Person to gain a fuller understanding of His good and perfect will. We must know His personality.

We are transformed by the renewing of our mind, and this is how we learn about the person of God. The promise in Romans 12:2 is that this process will enable us to discern the will of God. It happens by testing our will, and comparing it to our understanding of who He is.

For example, my wife and I have been married for over thirty-six years. During this time she has examined my personality and is able to discern my will. She no longer has to ask me if I would like ice cream on my pie. It may be polite to ask, but the answer is always going to be yes.

The more we know God, the more sure we become of His acceptable, good and perfect will. We can begin to anticipate his emotional response to a need, and in true relationship fashion, we share in that response. His heart is broken over the actions of a rebellious person, and our heart is moved to compassion as well.

We know from Scripture that He loves the widow, orphan and alien just as much as His chosen people. He wishes that they be cared for and welcomed. I know the answer He will give if I agree with Him in prayer and ask if I should take any action to meet their needs. It is His will! The answer is "Yes."

Jesus said that He could do nothing of His own accord, but only what He saw the Father doing (John 5:19). The Father is Jehovah-Rapha, the Healer, and so is Jesus the Son. It was Jesus that gave power and authority to the disciples to spread the work of healing. What He commanded them to do was His will, just as what He did was the Father's will.

> ...He gave them power and authority to drive out all demons and to cure diseases, and He sent them out to preach the kingdom of God and to heal the sick. - Luke 9:1-2

We know that His will is to free prisoners and the oppressed, and to recover sight for the blind, as stated in Luke 4, and that this is true in the physical, emotional and spiritual realms.

We know that it is His will to drive out all demons, to cure diseases, and to heal the sick.

Pray boldly for healing. Reconciliation is always God's will.

His Peculiar Will

Likewise the Spirit helps us in our weakness. For we do not know what to pray for as we ought, but the Spirit Himself intercedes for us with groanings too deep for words. And He who searches hearts knows what is the mind of the Spirit, because the Spirit intercedes for the saints according to the will of God. - Romans 8:26-27

God created order, but He is not confined by it. He created laws and consequences, but He controls outcomes. This is the basis on which miracles happen. God broke His own "law" by turning water into wine, making an iron ax-head float, and keeping three men from being consumed in an extremely hot fire. These are just a few examples of God's peculiar will. I use this word in the sense of His will being specific or particular to a situation or condition.

How can we possibly know the will of God, if He maintains the right to change it from time to time or situation to situation?

We can only know by coming into agreement with Him, and that takes communication and understanding. He knows that our mental capacity is too small for His ways, but He has given us the Spirit Himself to intercede for us when we don't know how to pray properly.

Paul describes the Spirit's intercession for us as groanings too deep for words. This is not to suggest that His prayer is hidden from our understanding. It means that the content is difficult to articulate. Yet, we can listen to the Spirit through our spirit and know God's peculiar will in the matter.

"For who has known the mind of the Lord that he may instruct Him?" But we have the mind of Christ. - 1 Corinthians 2:16

This verse means that we are not smart enough to tell the Lord what to do, but we are smart enough to receive any insight He is willing to give. When the Holy Spirit groans, I must listen.

For instance, I am asked to pray for many different kinds of people and situations. Sometimes I know the prayer strategy to take right away, such as driving out a demon. The power and authority has been given to drive them all out because they interrupt the reconciliation process that is God's declared will.

At other times I need to wait on God for a prayer strategy before I can intercede. I do this by praying in the Spirit, listening for His guidance, and thereby testing the peculiar will of God.

I can only confidently pray what matches up to God's will. When I know that, then I can pray boldly.

Battle of Wills

But He said to them, "You give them something to eat." They said, "We have no more than five loaves and two fish—unless we are to go and buy food for all these people." - Luke 9:13

No one can pray confidently when they are in a battle of wills with the Lord. It just doesn't make sense to go toe to toe with the Creator of the universe and hope to get your way. But God is merciful and loving, and His way is always better than my way.

There is an example of a battle of wills in the Gospel's account of feeding the multitudes. Jesus was clear about His will. He wanted the people to be fed. The disciples disagreed with His will (really!). It's not that they wanted the people to go hungry, but that they wanted to protect themselves from the responsibility of the mission. When they argued that they couldn't do it, they were also saying that they wouldn't do it.

A better response would have been:

"Jesus, I agree with You that these people need something to eat. I'd love to feed them, but I'm fresh out of ideas about how to go about it. What recommendations do You have?"

I encourage you to have the mind of Christ. Think His thoughts, feel His feelings, and desire the same things He desires. Pray confidently to expel all demons, cure disease, heal the sick,[13] free prisoners, release the oppressed,[14] feed the people,[15] feed His sheep,[16] and declare the Kingdom is here.[17] You may need to ask Him for fresh ideas about how to do it.

Surrender yourself in the battle of wills. As a reconciled servant and minister of Christ, you would never attempt to strong-arm God or out maneuver Him to get your own way. Yet when we instinctively operate in the physical here and now, rather than the spiritual and prophetic, our natural response, like the disciples, is to challenge the directives of God we find objectionable or unrealistic. Allow your strong faith to integrate your relationship with Him and you will experience supernatural prayers.

Listening Prayer

So faith comes from hearing, and hearing through the word of Christ. - Romans 10:17

There are times when a person needs to pour their heart out to the Lord, as David did in some of his Psalms. There are times when we recognize truth as we articulate it in prayer. But the most important part of healing prayer is to regularly check in with God. Only He can perform miracles, and He knows just how to go about it. When we pray, God wants us to hear our requests and listen to Him.[18] It makes all the difference.

It is appropriate to ask God a specific question and then listen for Him to give a specific answer. Generalities erode faith instead of building it.

When we engage in healing prayer, we usually ask God to reveal truth to the person with whom we are praying. When they hear a message from me it goes through their ears and into their brain where it is analyzed and interpreted through their frame of reference. This is a problem when their frame of reference distorts the truth to fit preconceived ideas. In addition, the typical mental response is to compare and consider information before accepting it, which is a repeat of the original sin - eating of the fruit of knowledge.

When God speaks to the person, on the other hand, it goes through their spirit into their core identity. It renews their mind by reconciling them to their identity in Christ. The person that hears a word from God in their heart believes it to be true in their heart.

I would rather the person hear one clear word from God than a whole dissertation from me, no matter how eloquently I am able to deliver it.

When we ask God a question there are several ways in which He may answer it.

We have noticed that the way God reveals truth to a person often corresponds to their primary learning style. Here are some examples in each of these styles of learning: visual, kinesthetic, auditory, and intuition. God also reveals truth through words of knowledge and prophecy, irrespective of learning style.

Visual

A visual learner, when hearing from God, may see a picture in his mind's eye. This picture is like a still shot that has meaning to him specific to the question asked. Some pictures are realistic, like a photograph, where others are more impressionistic. God has artistic ways to portray His message through these pictures.

Sometimes a visual person will see a vision in his mind's eye. A vision is more like a scene in a movie in that it includes action and a sense of progression. Ezekiel's visions fit into this category and demonstrate how visions can sometimes be interactive.

A vision may come to a person when they are sleeping, in which case we call it a dream. Sometimes God uses the relaxed state of sleep to slip a vision past the guardian brain.

Analytical and logical people often "explain away" a vision, but they may accept a dream that comes through the unguarded subconscious. However, not all dreams are revelations from God. We can accept truth from God through a dream, but should not try to fit God's truth into any or every dream we have.

Probably the most common way I have seen visual people receive truth from God is through memories. God calls to his or her mind a specific event, sometimes in great detail, because it represents a situation that requires mind renewal.

Rebecca, for example, came for prayer because her life was filled with rejection. When I asked God to reveal to her where this sense of rejection started, she suddenly got a shocked look on her face. I asked her what God had revealed.

"Oh, it's nothing," she stammered. "I just recalled something, but it was a long time ago. In fact, I haven't thought of that in years."

This is one of the best clues that the thought or memory is from God. Why else would someone think of it when asking for revelation, except that it was God's direct answer to a question?

Auditory

Another way God reveals truth is through sounds. In some cases, it is the voice of God speaking in words the person understands. The message is on point and consistent with His nature. I have asked more than once how the person knew it was God speaking. In every case the answer is: "Oh, it's God! There's no mistaking that."

One of my favorite examples of this was when my wife and I were praying with a woman who was in the midst of turmoil. Her life was upside down, and she was at her wit's end. She asked if God was big enough for the horrible mess she was in. We encouraged her to ask Him.

"God, are You big enough for this?!" she shouted in an angry tone.

Suddenly she got a very disgusted look on her face.

"What did He say?" my wife asked.

"All He said was: 'I am,'" she announced in a sarcastic tone.

But as the truth of those words seeped into her, she collapsed onto her couch and every ounce of tension evaporated from her body.

"He said, 'I AM!'" she cried. And that settled the matter for her.

Sometimes God will use the voice of authority. I do not mean a Hollywood version of James Earl Jones, but the voice of someone that held a position of authority over the person. For instance, it could be from a conversation they had with a parent, grandparent, teacher, elder, or pastor. It may be a new message coming through that trusted advisor's voice, or it may be a reminder of a word God spoke through that person before.

Another way God speaks to people is through Scripture. In a prayer appointment it is most often a specific verse memorized in their past that God calls back to their mind for consideration. This usually happens for people that have a Christian background or upbringing that gave them familiarity with the Bible, but I have also witnessed it in non-believers.

Kinesthetic

Kinesthetic learners are "hands on" people. They "get it" when they can experience it, feel it, and manipulate it. God speaks to kinesthetic learners through emotions and feelings.

When a person expects to see a vision or hear God speak to them, they may not know that He communicates through their emotions and feelings also. In these cases I sometimes prompt them by asking if they are experiencing a strong emotion, or if they felt an emotional shift.

All of a person's memories are available in their mind. A memory is associated with an event, and the two handles for that memory are *emotion* and *belief.* When something happens, large or small, we have an emotional response and our brain either reaffirms or establishes a belief. That is why God brings memories to one's mind for mind renewal. It gives opportunity to interrogate feelings and beliefs.

For example, if the prayer request is for God to show where a sense of rejection originates, then it is likely He will call to mind a memory in which the person began to believe she was rejected.

Sometimes God speaks through sensations. I once prayed with a young Christian man about his sense of abandonment. God had shown him the event in which he came to believe he was abandoned, so I followed that up with a request for truth to replace that belief.

After some time, I asked if God was showing him anything. He shook his head, so I asked if he was hearing anything. He shook his head again. I asked if he was getting anything at all, and again he indicated there was nothing.

"Do you feel anything?" I offered. "Any strong sensation or emotion?"

"Yes," he said. "I feel like God just picked me up and put me on His lap. He put a warm blanket around me, and is just holding me. It feels really good. Can I stay here for a while?"

God demonstrated His presence and love in that very tangible way, and it made all the difference to him.

One other way God reveals truth to people is through *body memories.* Physical scientists have discovered that memories are not just recorded in the brain, but some are stored in our body. When the memory is stirred up the nervous system has a reflex response.

A woman that had been physically abused suddenly felt like she could not breathe. That body memory brought her quickly to the place where Christ ministered to her original pain.

Insight

Sometimes the thoughts of God are unutterable because His ways are higher than our ways. He can reveal truth to us through insight. My friend describes this as "remembering something you never knew before." Another friend described it as "having a thought that is too smart to be mine." My own description is "to know something to be true that you did not arrive at through personal logic or reasoning."

Clint had one of these "aha moments" during a prayer time. He had suffered guilt and shame for many years because of egregious sins he had committed. He had asked for forgiveness many times, and though he claimed it by faith, he had not felt forgiven inside. I asked Jesus to reveal the truth to his heart.

"It's fine now. I'm OK." He said matter-of-factly.

This issue had been such a pervasive one that I pressed in and asked how he knew it was "fine now," when he had been plagued by guilt and shame for so long.

"Jesus did it."

I could tell he was speaking from his heart and not his head. For years he had tried to force the truth in through his mind, but now it was true in his heart. The truth is the truth, and the shift in his thinking was permanent - complete without effort.

As subtle as an "aha moment" can be, a much more dramatic form of insight is an epiphany. The connotation of epiphany is to "see the light" or to come to a supernatural understanding through direct influence of God. Saul experienced this while on his way to Damascus. The blinding light and voice of thunder underscored the importance of the message.

Whether the insight is subtle or dramatic, it is recognized as truth because it comes from God. Contrast this with an intuition or gut feeling that a person holds on impulse, which originates from the person's mind, and may or may not be trustworthy. The truth, the other hand, resonates with the Spirit, is completely reliable, and has eternal implications.

Word of Knowledge

There are times when the Holy Spirit reveals truth through a word of knowledge so that a person knows something even though there is no earthly explanation for how he knows it. Several times in the gospels this is described of Jesus as he knew what the Pharisees were thinking, what the disciples were arguing about, or how much faith a person had.

If you receive a word of knowledge as the intercessor, wait for permission from the Spirit to share it. It is given for direction and to build faith.

Test for direction. Why did God give the word of knowledge? Imagine that a prayer for healing seems stuck and the recipient is not able to hear from God. A word of knowledge may disclose an offender in the recipient's life that needs to be forgiven, a sin that needs to be confessed, or some other barrier that needs to be removed. Introduce what has been revealed and ask for permission to pray in that direction.

Share the word of knowledge to build faith. Imagine a setting in which you introduce something that you could not possibly know except that it was revealed by the Spirit. The recipient would have increased confidence that God is speaking through you, and that your role in the prayer time is to facilitate their conversation with God about a specific subject.

I have seen God open conversations through a word of knowledge that would not have happened outside of that divine revelation.

Share the word to confirm the truth. I have received a word of knowledge in a prayer appointment that needed to be held back for a time. The recipient was unsure about what he was hearing from the Lord. After he shared what he thought he heard, I was able to confirm the message having already received the same message. Exercising his own hearing helped his faith grow; having the message confirmed by me built his confidence.

Another form of divine information is a prophetic word. Where a word of knowledge has to do with information, a prophetic word is a message from God. Specifically, to prophesy is to speak the word of God for Him. There is power in the spoken word, and it is a privilege to be entrusted with the word of God.

It takes experience operating in the prophetic to learn when and how God wants you to share His word. For instance, in the story of the valley of dry bones (Ezekiel 37) God tells Ezekiel to prophesy. As Ezekiel obeys the command of the Lord, the bones come to life. Being entrusted with God's powerful word is an important stewardship.

סלה

God uses many means to reveal His truth to the one that seeks Him. It is His will to communicate with us because we are created in His image for relationship with Him. Just ask and listen for His voice in a whisper, wind, fire, storm or any other way He chooses.

"Why is it so hard for me to hear God?" Tim demanded. "If He wants me to know something, why doesn't He come right out and say it?"

"Are you wondering why God doesn't knock you off your donkey like Saul on the road to Damascus,[19] or use signs and wonders like the Plagues in Egypt,[20] or open your eyes to the spiritual realm like Elisha's servant?[21]" I asked to clarify.

Tim thought for a moment and then answered: "Well, maybe not quite that dramatic, but something more than a whisper or nudge would be nice."

"What if God loves you so much, that He communicates in whispers and nudges instead?" I asked rhetorically.

There is a balance and order in the universe God created. Imagine that the devil demands the right to communicate with you in the same way that God does. God uses signs and wonders, or a booming voice, or a blinding light, or revelation of the spiritual realm, or miracles that override natural law -

but only in the most loving ways. If the devil had unlimited access to those it would be very dangerous.

God's love keeps us from being in harm's way. We can learn to *discern* subtle truths, affirmations, and directions from God just as we can learn to *withstand* subtle lies, accusations, and deceptions from His enemy. The devil would welcome the chance to use a booming voice to broadcast accusations, signs and wonders to mislead, or visions of demonic forces to abuse us through our unredeemed nature of fear and greed.

"Be thankful that God trusts you with subtle whispers," I encouraged Tim. "God speaks with increasing directness to those who know Him and have learned to recognize His voice because they are not as susceptible to the wiles of the enemy."

The Power of God

> *Truly, truly, I say to you, whoever believes in Me will also do the works that I do; and greater works than these will he do, because I am going to the Father. - John 14:12*

The most important aspect of healing prayer is to understand that all the power for healing and miracles comes from God the Father.

Jesus told the disciples that anyone who believes in Him would do the works that He did, and greater works also. Then the verse continues by saying: "because I am going to the Father." While Jesus was with them they were able to do the works that He did, as recorded in Luke 10. He went on to assure them that they would receive another Comforter, the Holy Spirit, because He was going to the Father.

Watch the path of authority, or chain of command, because nothing can happen without proper permission:

God is creator of all things and has complete authority over life, death, sickness, health, and all things in all realms. The Old Testament includes many miracles and healings done through the authority of God by His appointed priest, prophet or king.

Jesus came as Son of God and Son of Man, and every miracle He did was through the authority of God the Father. The path of authority was always through God the Father. Jesus sent the disciples out on a mission, having given them authority passed through Him from God the Father. In that authority they were able to cast out demons, cure diseases, and heal the sick. When Jesus ascended into heaven, He sent the Holy Spirit to link the disciples to the authority of God the Father.

When we pray for healing, cast out demons, cure diseases, and heal sicknesses it is with the post-Pentecost authority that the apostles demonstrated.

It is our mission to bring the good news of the gospel, as Jesus did, and to demonstrate it with power.

Chapter Four:
The Human Construct

So God created man in His own image, in the image of God He created him; male and female He created them. - Genesis 1:27

God made mankind to reflect His image and character. This is hard to understand because God is a spirit. He does not have a physical body, yet He created us as spiritual beings that exist in a body of flesh and blood.

He created us with three distinct components: body, soul and spirit. Each is separate, yet like the Trinity, all three are interrelated, and like the Trinity, we can focus our attention on one component but never at the exclusion of the other components.

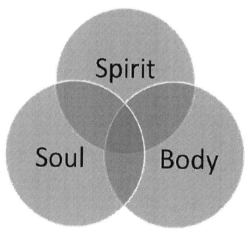

This diagram represents the three parts and how they interact. Each part is distinct, yet overlaps the others. If the three circles were perfectly aligned, looking like a single circle, it would represent the totally integrated person.

Conversely, if the circles spread so they no longer overlap they would represent a dis-integrated person.

The parts are important to understand because they have unique roles and functions in each person's life. We look at the Designer's purpose for each and then consider this model for gaining wholeness and healing.

Body

> *Then the LORD God formed the man of dust from the ground ... - Genesis 2:7*

God made the physical body out of dust. He took parts of the earth, atoms and molecules, and repurposed them in an organized way. The structure and function of the parts of the human body allow for interaction with other physical elements.

The body operates according to the five senses: taste, touch, sight, smell, and sound. Through these portals we have awareness of our surroundings. These are the special gifts that allow the body to interact with the world.

I do not know much about angels and demons, except that they are created beings that inhabit the spiritual realm. They interact with the physical realm, but on a very limited basis. Fallen angels, also called demons or unclean spirits, apparently need a host body so they can interact with the world. For instance, a demon cannot carry and detonate a bomb vest, but a demon possessed person can carry out this evil act.

God's original plan is expressed by His blessing to Adam and Eve immediately following their creation.

> *And God blessed them. And God said to them, "Be fruitful and multiply and fill the earth and subdue it, and have dominion over the fish of the sea and over the birds of the heavens and over every living thing that moves on the earth." - Genesis 1:28*

The assignment was to fill, subdue and have dominion over the physical earth. Certainly God has the authority and power to fill, subdue and have dominion over the earth. He proved that with the acts of creation. For some divine reason He chose to invite mankind to participate in this plan. It is a masterful plan!

What if God wanted to enjoy creation through the eyes of a child? It would bring Him pleasure to experience the wonders of nature from a completely different perspective.

Imagine a father taking his child to the zoo to see exotic animals. Each new creature would elicit gasps of excitement and oohs of amazement because of their color, size, shape or actions. The father would remember the first time he saw a duckbilled platypus. He would giggle with the child's delight over the antics of a monkey. That is how I imagine the interaction between God and Adam during the naming of the animals (Genesis 2:19.)

Man was given another purpose to perform on earth, the God-given assignment to be a steward over the entire physical realm. Yet God did not create man, place him on the earth with the assignment, and then step back to objectively watch the experiment unfold. He gave man the responsibility and the authority with which to carry it out, and He gave him something more.

Spirit

> ... and breathed into his nostrils the breath of life ... -
> Genesis 2:7

The "Breath of Life" is the Holy Spirit, or more specifically, a replication and multiplication of Him inside of man. God became life inside of man, and the spirit of man was as united to the Spirit of God as a husband is to a wife. They were one in spirit, and one Spirit.

God and man communicated Spirit to spirit. This was like a data link of uninterrupted information between them by which man knew the heart of God. It was the communication link through which God experienced His creation from Adam's perspective. Like a perfect union, there was complete agreement between them: no competition for desires, opinions, or feelings, nor demand to express them. God's will and Adam's were in total harmony.

Then came sin. Man chose to divorce God, to reject the Spirit within, and took on the responsibility to determine good and evil. This was not part of Adam's original mandate or purpose. God had been the one to identify what was good and what was not good. Man was not designed for that task, and had no authority to make his judgments stick. It was an assumed responsibility that continues to be filled with conflict.

Thank God for Pentecost as the fulfilment of the promise that He would restore the connection. The Spirit fills the accepting believer and restores the communication link between God and man.

Soul

... and the man became a living creature. - Genesis 2:7

Genesis records that man became a living (*alive*) creature (*person*).

Alive means to have life. In biology it refers to an organism, the smallest unit of life, which is one or more cells that undergo metabolism, has a program for self-regulation and is capable of reproduction. In other words it can grow, respond to stimuli, and adapt to its environment.

A *person* is conscious of self, has continuity of identity, initiates relationships, and is able to make choices. In other words, he is aware that he exists, has existed, and expects to exist in the future. He differentiates self from his surroundings and other persons. He can make choices that affect the way he relates with others.

The *soul* consists of the mind, will and emotions which control what a person thinks, wants and feels. It is the control center for personhood and identity. A body can be alive as defined above, but it must have a soul to become a person.

Originally the soul and spirit were in complete harmony. The spirit was the communication link with God and the soul was the communication link with the body and physical realm. Sights, sounds, smells, touch and taste came through the body to the soul and from the soul to the spirit.

What God thought, felt, desired and spoke were transferred to man from Spirit to spirit, spirit to soul, and soul to body. Since everything was in perfect harmony there were no glitches or interruptions in the connection. God could influence man without hindrance, and vice versa.

Then sin caused a divorce between God and man, between Spirit and spirit. Man became afraid of God and felt the burden of responsibility for the knowledge of good and evil. Without the Spirit of God to guide him, man's spirit atrophied. The soul became the seat of judgment in place of the spirit-link to God, and man began to rely on his mind, will and emotions to determine good and evil. The soul also abandoned the spirit as a source of trustworthy information and took on sole responsibility for the personality.

We use this saying in our teaching and ministry: You are who God says you are. That is your *true identity*. But you are being who you believe you are. That is your *active identity*.

Taking a closer look at the components of the soul, we see that the mind, will and emotions are prone to error. The rogue soul operates independently from God and is obsessed with self-preservation. The *mind* collects and recalls data that it has arranged according to patterns and conclusions. This is the paradigm, or what you believe to be true. The *will* makes choices and calls forth action, thereby dictating behavior. The *emotions* provide a feedback loop and are used as a handle for memories and other bits of information.

This potentially unredeemed soul develops and guards the personality and identity of the person.

Whenever there is a disagreement between who you are being and who God says you are, there is conflict. Where that conflict exists there is pain, and that pain points to the place where healing needs to happen. When the conflict is resolved we are reconciled to God through Christ. Healing is the outcome of that reconciliation.

Three Realms

God created us to operate in three distinct realms: spiritual, emotional and physical. Each realm corresponds to its functional context as described above: Body = physical; Soul = emotional; Spirit = spiritual. We cannot accept one realm and deny the existence of the others, because God designed them to interact with each other.

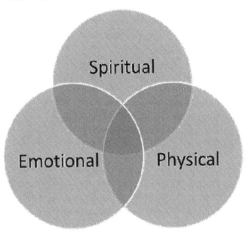

In this diagram we show the realms overlapping to depict the influence that each has over the others. For instance, something that happens in the spiritual realm will have a direct bearing on the emotional and physical realms. We may be able to identify the originating realm, but the outcome will be expressed in the other realms as well.

A total integration could be represented by a convergence of the three circles. In this scenario, input in one realm would completely and immediately influence the other realms. There would be no distinction or isolation between them. For instance, a cause in the spiritual realm would have an immediate effect in the physical and emotional realms.

Divergence between the realms temporarily isolates the cause and effect to a specific realm. For example, a "cause" in the physical realm (body) such as a sexual sin will manifest an "effect" in that same realm such as a venereal disease. However, God designed the body to be integrated, and sooner or later the effect will manifest in the other realms as well. Therefore the physical act of sexual sin will have consequences in the emotional and spiritual realms, such as broken relationships, guilt, and separation.

Scripture backs this up. Paul writes in 1 Corinthians 6:15-20 that sin with a prostitute joins their bodies together (physical), that the two are joined together as one (emotional), and that the sin is against the Spirit because the body is His temple (spiritual).

This has a big impact on healing, because a pain or problem is not limited to one realm or the other. Although a need may manifest in one realm more readily than the others, it will influence the whole person over time.

Let us look at a person that is addicted to alcohol from the perspective of each of the realms. God sees the person as a whole, while the Western worldview sees him as the sum of the parts. We will look at the parts and then draw them back into a whole.

The *physical realm* is the most common lens to reality in western culture. A scientist or doctor may explain that alcohol is a chemical that affects some more than others, depending on their genetic makeup. There are hereditary factors that predispose a person toward alcoholism. Additionally, the body of an alcoholic has a chemical imbalance. Each of these factors can be measured and tested.

If sufficient knowledge were available, a corrective combination of remedies could be used to cure the problem.

For instance, a man was introduced to alcohol in his early teens by an older family member. His repetitive drinking caused a physical reaction and now his body craves it. The apparent solution is to force the body into a rebalance by eliminating future alcohol either cold-turkey or in some measured way. Once the imbalance is corrected the problem should be solved.

In other words, a scientist or doctor limits treatment to the measurable symptoms of the problem in the physical realm. If that is not effective, he assumes there is no solution.

The *emotional realm* is unseen but its existence is widely accepted. Counselors and therapists are examples of those most likely to view the condition through the lens of the emotional realm. They may consider that alcohol is the person's solution to an emotional trauma or negative feeling, and believe that some temperaments and personality types are more susceptible to such addictive behavior. The root cause of the problem is unseen, they believe, but works in the emotional center of the person's identity. Their solution is to find new and healthy ways for the person to feel, think, and act.

For instance, a veteran returned from a war zone with traumatic images and memories from his experience. He abuses alcohol in an effort to quiet the pain or distance himself from the feelings. Their solution is to desensitize him to the trauma or convert the memories in other ways. Once the emotional pain is neutralized the problem should be solved.

In other words, a counselor or therapist treats the condition in the emotional realm in a way that overcomes the trauma, or exchanges one way of thinking for another. The counselor or therapist may not be equipped to address the other realms.

The *spiritual realm* is widely accepted as a valid lens to reality in some cultures, but virtually ignored in the West. In the spiritual realm alcoholism is seen as an outcome of unclean spirits, such as the demon alcohol. It can be the result of a curse or hex. A person can bring it on himself through a rash oath or vow, or by making an illicit agreement with the devil. Pastors and spiritual advisers are the ones most likely to frame alcoholism in terms of the spiritual realm.

For instance, a woman struggled with alcohol since high school, and was completely under its power. Her father and mother also fought against the power of addiction, and always feared that she would not escape its grasp. On his deathbed it was discovered that her grandfather was a closet alcoholic. The pastor realized that she was set up for failure from the start because of the generational curse that had been passed down. The pastor cast out the demon alcohol and broke the curse to set her free from the addiction.

In other words, a pastor will treat this condition in the spiritual realm by using spiritual authority and divine power to overcome the stronghold of the devil.

Therefore, if anyone is in Christ, he is a new creation. The old has passed away; behold, the new has come. - 2 Corinthians 5:17

Complete healing happens when the person is reconciled to God through Christ, the realms are integrated, and that person becomes a new creation. This kind of healing works from the inside out.

My wife had been praying with a woman named Sydney off and on for a few months. The Holy Spirit guided the prayer sessions into times of confession and repentance, times of forgiving and being forgiven, and times of mind renewal where Sydney replaced false beliefs with God's truth. The transformation was amazing.

One day Sydney expressed great discouragement, and through her tears asked: "Why won't God heal my back? I've asked Him to take away this chronic pain, but He hasn't. Is there something wrong with me? Is He unwilling to heal me physically?"

My wife responded: "I believe God healed you in the spiritual realm right when you asked Him to forgive. I believe God healed you in the emotional realm, and you've received joy in place of sorrow and peace in place of turmoil. I believe He has healed you completely, and I don't know why it hasn't yet manifested in the physical realm. But since you're healed in the other realms, I think you can claim physical healing also."

In less than a week the pain in her back was completely gone. The healing did manifest in the physical realm because it was complete healing.

In another example, I had opportunity to pray with a man that struggled with addiction to alcohol for many years. He readily walked through asking for and extending forgiveness, and then I prayed that he be healed from alcoholism.

Much to the surprise of his coworkers and family, God took away his dependence on alcohol. He had no withdrawal symptoms, no medical issues, and no desire to go back to it. This physical healing gave him opportunity to deal with the emotional pain and spiritual strongholds that were at the root of the behavior.

The Holy Spirit guides the healing process. When we follow His lead it produces reconciliation from one realm to another until the process is complete. The person becomes a new creature in Christ, and their God-given identity is released.

We must follow His master plan.

Chapter Five:
Spiritual Realm

For we do not wrestle against flesh and blood, but against the rulers, against the authorities, against the cosmic powers over this present darkness, against the spiritual forces of evil in the heavenly places. - Ephesians 6:12

In Jesus' day, every calamity, every illness, every disease and every curse was associated with unclean spirits. There was no surprise to the disciples that they were given authority over demons and then told to heal the sick and cure diseases. They understood that those things were related.

The spiritual is the unseen realm. It includes the heavenly places where Christ is with God and angels,[22] but is also inhabited by rulers, authorities, cosmic powers, and spiritual forces of evil.[23] Through these the devil subjects people to lifelong slavery by the fear of death, as it says in Hebrews 2:14-15. But this same Scripture says that Jesus Christ's death destroyed the devil in the prophetic tense.

We wrestle against these spiritual powers and forces by understanding authority and our rights as the ones that bear God's image.

We test for wholeness in the spiritual realm with discernment and the conscience. The opposite of wholeness is marked by broken relationships with God and others, feelings of guilt or shame, strongholds, torments, and unconfessed or hidden sin.

Authority

And His disciples asked Him, "Rabbi, who sinned, this man or his parents, that he was born blind?" - John 9:2

Every time a person sins, it transfers authority to the devil. Every time a sin is forgiven, it transfers authority back.

The disciples understood the relationship between sin and consequences. When they saw the man that was born blind, it was the perfect opportunity to learn more about wielding authority. They asked the question of Jesus, wanting to trace consequences back to the source of the pain. I am defending the disciples' right to ask the question, because it is wise to get to the bottom of the problem that you are praying to resolve.

Jesus did not rebuke the disciples for their question, nor did He say that the man and his parents were without sin. They had asked if it was his sin or his parents' sin, so Jesus replied that they were asking the wrong question. The risk is that the answer leads to blame. Instead, they should have asked "What is the purpose of his blindness?" Jesus responded to the unasked question by explaining his blindness was a precursor to miraculous healing.

When we are investigating a sickness, disease or oppression of any kind, as intercessors we often search for the root of the problem. We also look to find who sinned, not so we have someone to blame but so we know who to forgive.

Warren struggled with pornography for many years. As we went to prayer, God revealed that he was most vulnerable when he was lonely or frustrated. Then we asked God to reveal the origin of this problem.

Warren recalled the day he discovered adult magazines in his dad's bedroom. He was a curious eleven-year-old boy at the time. During his teen years his parents were gone a lot, so he spent more and more of his time looking at the pictures. He was addicted before he left home, and the internet made it impossible to break the habit.

He was oppressed by an unclean spirit. Warren had given authority to the spirit of *porneo* to help him deal with loneliness. The sin of engaging in pornography was the decision that transferred authority to the devil.

I helped Warren see that it was sinful for him to choose pornography, and that he was responsible for that choice over and over again, ever since his teen years. He confessed the sin and received forgiveness.

Then I helped him see that it was wrong for his dad to allow his innocence to be destroyed in that way. It was wrong for him to have that kind of temptation in the home, and it was wrong for both his parents to be unavailable to address his curiosity. He willingly forgave his dad and mom for those offenses.

Having removed that authority from the devil through receiving and giving forgiveness, it was easy to evict the spirit of *porneo* in the name of the Lord Jesus, and to demand that it never return. Warren was immediately set free in the spiritual realm.

> *And Jesus came and said to them, "All authority in heaven and on earth has been given to Me. Go therefore ... And behold, I am with you always, to the end of the age." - Matthew 28:18-20*

These verses make it very clear that Jesus was given all authority in heaven and on earth. That means He has the right to rule in the physical, emotional and spiritual realms. It covers everything.

Jesus has the authority to override your free will, but He never will because it would be a violation of unconditional love. To override another's free will is abuse.

Satan does not have the authority to override your free will, but he will do anything he can to deceive you into giving him authority. Once you have transferred authority, he will abuse you with it.

Jesus is sinless. He has authority over the devil and always will because there will never be a circumstance in which His perfection can be questioned. That was the victory He won both in the wilderness and in the Garden of Gethsemane.

The verse quoted above states that Jesus will be with us always, to the end of the age. It is the presence of God, through Jesus, and by the Holy Spirit within us that gives us access to His authority.

When a person is given an order, the chain of command requires that the one issuing the order have the authority to accomplish the command. For example, a man does not have the authority to take the life of another man. God does have that authority. If God commands you to take the life of another man, you have the right to do so through a transfer of God's authority, specific to that order. For instance, He commanded "*Whoever blasphemes the name of the LORD shall surely be put to death*."[24] When you are "under orders" the chain of command compels, empowers, and protects you.

Jesus has been given all authority, and from that perspective He says: "Go therefore ..." He has given authority to baptize, teach, and make disciples.

> "*Behold, I have given you authority to tread on serpents and scorpions, and over all the power of the enemy, and nothing shall hurt you.* - Luke 10:19

When we take authority over an unclean spirit, we do so in Jesus' name. That is a reminder that we are acting under His orders. The demons and all the power of the enemy must surrender to His authority.

After I prayed with Warren, I helped him understand his authority as a forgiven believer. He has the right to cast out the spirit of *porneo* in the name of Jesus, just as I did. This reminder helped him hold the territory, because an unclean spirit may return to tempt and try to deceive.

Legal Ground

> *The sting of death is sin, and the power of sin is the law.* - 1 Corinthians 15:56

Satan is the ultimate legalist. The law, when it is devoid of love, is a tool for controlling others and a shortcut against relationship. As this verse says, the power of sin is the law because it defines judgment and condemnation. Satan wields the law to pronounce death.

God gave the law, and as the Psalmist writes, His law is perfect. That is because God is love, and His purpose is redemption rather than death. Once sin entered into the human race, the law became a death sentence because it correctly identified man's rebellion against God. The antidote to sin according to the law is forgiveness according to God's mercy.

It is helpful to know the law to avoid being ensnared by it. That is why we need an Advocate at the judgment throne who will render true justice, properly accounting for God's work of reconciliation through the cross.

Satan does not tell the truth about the law. He is the father of lies, and has been a liar from the beginning. His motive is to destroy relationships, especially between God and His creation. He uses the law to accomplish his abuse.

Let me share a personal story about law and intimidation. One afternoon a man knocked on my front door and handed me a large envelope, saying 'You've been served.' My wife asked what it was that needed this special delivery, and I answered that it was some legal paperwork.

It was a letter from a local attorney addressed to me and my wife that alleged illegal activity on our part. It advised us that a lawsuit would begin against us, as well as criminal charges. We had thirty days to respond or the case would move ahead. It was very intimidating.

The main charge was that I had been involved in a hit and run accident nearly two years before, and the driver of the van I hit was seeking settlement.

The next day I faxed a reply to the attorney's office. On the cover sheet I drew a picture of a tree and a dog in full hue and cry. I labeled the dog with the attorney's name. I labeled the tree: "The Wrong Tree." Included in the package was a copy of the accident report submitted by the County Sheriff at the time of the accident.

I knew the law. I knew my rights under the law. The charges and allegations were threatening, but unfounded. There was no basis in them. The attorney was barking up the wrong tree. We heard nothing from him after that.

The Holy Spirit guides our spirit and directs us with specific orders. When we obey Him, we are "under orders" and the authority to accomplish His directive has been given through Jesus. This is the confidence we have when engaged in spiritual warfare against the defeated foe.

> *For the weapons of our warfare are not of the flesh but have divine power to destroy strongholds. We destroy arguments and every lofty opinion raised against the knowledge of God, and take every thought captive to obey Christ ... - 2 Corinthians 10:4-6*

A stronghold is something that contradicts the word of God. The enemy uses strongholds to mount an attack against God's defenses. When these lies are believed by a person, the devil is able to claim legal ground through which to enter.

For instance, a works-based salvation is a stronghold that proclaims the only way to please God is by what you do for Him. It is the idea that salvation is earned, rather than a gift. The person who believes this lie has opened the door to the accusations of the devil. They are condemned by their own standards and are enslaved to this stronghold.

The weapons of our warfare have the Holy Spirit guidance system installed. Truth finds its target and destroys it every time.

A temptation is a potential stronghold. Temptations are ideas or thoughts that draw us away from God. Be aware that the sting of temptation is in what it draws you away from, not in the bait used to entice you. Temptations are planted thoughts, often in the form of a question. For example: "Did God actually say, 'You shall not eat of any tree in the garden'?"

We overcome temptation and other thoughts by *taking them captive to obey Christ.*

Larry suffered from low self-esteem. We had prayed for guidance and the Holy Spirit revealed to him that he believed there was something fundamentally wrong with him. This was the thought that needed to be taken captive.

"Lord," I prayed. "Larry believes there is something wrong with him, that he is defective. Would you please reveal the truth to him?"

"I saw Jesus smiling at me!" Larry said. "He looked at me with approval, like I'm not defective at all!"

That's an example of taking a thought captive and making it obedient to Christ. We hold the thought up to the Light, and everything that is true resonates with the Light, but everything that is faulty is quickly exposed. The dispelled temptation or destroyed stronghold breaks the leverage of the legal ground.

There may be times when you sense a barrier to healing, and it is not apparent what legal ground the devil is claiming. When that happens you have the right to demand disclosure from him.

This happened to me while praying with a young man that was being demonized. I commanded the demon to leave in the name of the Lord, but it resisted. It told the young man that it did not have to leave, and that I could not force it to go.

I first asked the man if the demon was welcome there, because if it was then it had permission to stay. He declared firmly that the demon was not welcome.

Then I turned my attention to the demon and told it to state its case. I asked it under what authority it was resisting the command of Jesus. It refused to say.

"Because you have not adequately defended your authority, we demand that you leave in the name of Jesus Christ!" I said firmly, and it left.

Curses, Oaths and Vows

I tell you, on the Day of Judgment people will give account for every careless word they speak, - Matthew 12:36

We were created to reflect God's character and our words have creative power. Our words can be used to prophetically proclaim good, which is to bless. Though we lost our perfect reflection of God's character, our words still have creative power. They can be used to prophetically call forth harm, which is to curse. That is why Jesus warned so emphatically that an account will have to be given on the Day of Judgment.

What would cause a person to curse another? Hatred, anger and fear. Curses are rooted in sin. God cursed the serpent and the ground in response to sin,[25] but He has not asked man to curse for Him.[26] We curse out of pain and are generally not in agreement with God's perfect will.[27] Satan uses man's curses as authority, or legal ground, to stir up evil in our lives.

There are some curses that are placed on purpose. Some religious practices, such as voodoo, are founded in this kind of curse. Some groups and organizations use curses to force compliance or maintain secrets. The Bible also describes some people that curse because they do not fear God.

Other curses are placed unintentionally. People regularly pronounce curses without thinking, just because they are not sensitive to their power. They treat a curse like an audible emoticon or a meaningless expression of frustration. They even curse themselves! The devil will use a curse to his advantage whether it is intentional or not.

Curses can be broken off by appealing to a Higher Authority. In other words, the person that uttered the curse has done so on their authority. We identify the curse, and then appeal to God as the Highest Authority, and ask Him to revoke it. There may be legal ground associated with the curse that also requires forgiveness, either for the one under the curse or the one who uttered it. Claim and proclaim the forgiveness as appropriate, and then in the name of Jesus you can declare that the curse is null and void.

> ... *For I the LORD your God am a jealous God, visiting the iniquity of the fathers on the children to the third and the fourth generation of those who hate me, but showing steadfast love to thousands of those who love me and keep my commandments.* - Exodus 20:5-6

This is the Scripture that describes *generational curses.* It is God's warning that when a father sins, it is not just his life that is affected. His children and grandchildren will also suffer from the consequences. Examples of generational curses can be alcoholism and other addictions, cancer, diabetes, heart disease, or other "hereditary" conditions.

Generational curses are broken off by forgiving the parents, grandparents, and sometimes great-grandparents for passing along the sin. When the person under the curse is also forgiven for their role in the curse, they are able to appeal to a Higher Authority. God will forgive when we forgive, and when the sin has been reconciled in that way it no longer has power to pass the consequences to future generations. We can declare that the generational curse is broken and no longer has authority in that family line. It is declared null and void in the name of Jesus.

Blessings replace curses. I discovered that a blessing always overpowers a curse because God's will is that we bless. In His words: "Bless and curse not.[28]" When we break a curse and declare it null and void, it is appropriate to ask the Holy Spirit for the blessing that takes its place.

If you run into a curse that seems to be persistent, and you have trouble finding the root of it, then bless over top of it. There may be a war in the heavenlies because of it, but we can be confident that blessings overcome curses.

An *oath* is a binding promise you make to someone else. It has power in the spiritual realm. For instance, in a court room you may be asked to take an oath. You swear, with God as your judge, to tell the whole truth and nothing but the truth. Some consider this an empty ritual because they do not recognize God as an authority in their life, but the devil uses an oath to his advantage regardless of whether we take the oath seriously or not. If the person does not accept God as their judge, the devil fills the authority void and brings volumes of accusations and charges.[29]

Another example is when a person swears to another while holding himself as his highest authority. When a person says "I promise you" an "or else ..." is implied. The promise is balanced against a consequence, such as "I promise you or I will make restitution," or "I promise you or I'll die trying." The devil loves to fill in the blank, and will hold the person accountable to every evil thing he can squeeze into that space.

Oaths are broken off by appealing to a Higher Authority. As with curses, there may be offenses that need to be confessed and forgiven before the legal ground can be removed. Once that has happened, the person can retract the oath.

A *vow* is a binding promise you make to yourself that has power in the spiritual realm. Like an oath, it is a promise that the devil will hold you to.

Alex came for prayer because he was frustrated with his relationship with God. He had been clean and sober for nearly two years, and felt like God had been the One to rescue him. No matter what he tried, it was as if he could not have a close relationship with God. His prayers seemed empty and his spirit was dull.

I asked the Lord if there was any legal ground that the enemy was claiming to keep Alex from having a real relationship with Him.

"Oh my goodness," Alex exclaimed. "I just remembered one night when I was fourteen. I was already into marijuana and alcohol, and experimenting with some other drugs. It was a tough time in my life, my grandpa died, and my family was chaotic. I was out walking that night, and I was mad at God for letting all this stuff happen. I yelled out 'I will never trust You again!'"

That was it! He had made a rash vow, promising to never trust God again. Now the devil was holding him to his promise. Every time he tried to put his faith in God, the accuser blocked him. It was as if the devil was saying: "You can't trust God, you promised you never would, and I'm holding you to your promise."

I asked Alex if he was willing to repent of that vow and ask God for forgiveness. He quickly agreed and we went to prayer. As we appealed to God as the Higher Authority, Alex felt the vow evaporate. I was able to bless him with a spiritual gift of faith to replace that rash vow.

In the years since that prayer time, Alex has demonstrated the gift of supernatural faith many times. He now serves the Lord in full time ministry, praying with people that are held captive by alcohol, drugs and other addictions.

Praise the Lord!

Chapter Six:
Emotional Realm

The emotional realm is the core of our personality and active identity. It is governed by our soul through what we think, want, and feel. This is the part of the human construct that measures "aliveness." An emotionally healthy person is glad to be alive, whereas an unhealthy one seeks death. This is the reason destructive behavior accompanies emotional distress. The addict, for instance, believes he is better off dead and uses drugs to commit suicide slowly and gradually.

The conflict between who you are being and who God created you to be is most evident in the emotional realm. The spiritual realm is mysterious and hidden until the Day of Judgment, and the physical realm uses all manner of coping strategies to mask the truth. But the emotional realm is the heart of your identity, and any difference between your active identity and your true identity can be found here.

The symptoms, or evidence, of conflict in the emotional realm include feelings and beliefs of sadness, disappointment, rejection, depression, grief, resentment, shame, frustration, rage, anger, failure, worthlessness, fear, anxiety, hopelessness, poverty, dependency, loneliness, lust, pride, envy, insecurity, timidity, and confusion.

You Are What You Believe

How you think, and what you believe to be true, determines how you view yourself. Your belief system governs your thoughts and becomes the framework through which you make choices, respond to situations, and express your personality. Your paradigm, or frame of reference, has been building since childhood, and the conclusions you made in the past affect how you see yourself and the world around you today.

What makes you be who you are? It begins with what you observe.

```
OBSERVE >
```

Even before your earliest memories, your body has been observing its surroundings and taking in information. Your senses feed a constant stream of input to your mind which enter consciously and subconsciously as observable facts, events and circumstances. Each new bit of information is compared to an existing body of knowledge, which I'm calling your *frame of reference*.

```
OBSERVE >   INTERPRET >
```

The next step is interpretation in which the observations are checked for accuracy and consistency. This energy-intensive process is a burden of the original sin where mankind took on the responsibility to decide if a bit of information is good or evil, true or false. This work would be a monumental task if the brain did not take shortcuts.

The first efficiency of the brain is to accept, without further scrutiny, any item that has already been decided. In other words, something that is believed to be true is automatically vetted and added to the preexisting conclusions that make up the frame of reference.

The second step is to accept information based on matching or mismatching patterns in the frame of reference. In other words, an item that appears similar to a previously decided one is accepted with the same conclusion.

All observed items that cannot be quickly categorized as good or evil must then be scrutinized. The default conclusion is that something new is evil, false, or harmful because your fallen nature operates on a basis of fear. You are prejudiced toward risk aversion for safety's sake.

Through this process you accumulate a belief system about what is good, true, or safe compared to what is evil, false, or dangerous.

OBSERVE 〉 INTERPRET 〉 BELIEVE 〉

You are what you believe, and over time your biases and judgments harden with a "preponderance of evidence" from conclusions that are self-fulfilling.

The mind cannot tolerate conflict between existing conclusions, your frame of reference, and new data. The creative subconscious will go to great lengths to resolve any such conflict.

If you believe that you are unlovable, then you will assume all new information supports that conclusion. For instance, if you observe two people whispering in the back of the room, your brain interprets this as gossip, and you conclude that they are talking negatively about you. It is a "natural" conclusion because you are unlovable.

On the other hand, if you observe something that seems to conflict with what you believe, then your mind will resolve the conflict in favor of your frame of reference. For example, if your pastor tells you that he loves you, your mind will interpret that as a harmless platitude from a man that is commanded to love everyone, even an unlovable one like you. Your conclusion supports your frame of reference that you are still unlovable, though you are willing to give your pastor credit for trying to obey the law.

The mind will not tolerate an open loop that exists when it cannot resolve a conflict. When its creative abilities are exhausted it will suppress the data until some future time when other resources might be available. For example, a suppressed memory is an event that is stored inaccessibly in the brain. In some cases it cannot be recalled at all, and in other cases it is a vague memory. It is as if a label has been put on it that reads: "I can't know."

What you believe to be true acts as if it is true to you because your brain fulfills what it believes.

The way you feel, your emotional response, is determined by what you believe. Feelings are an indication of being alive, and collectively they express your personality, frame of reference, and identity.

For example, you feel rejected because you believe you are unloved. You feel angry because you believe someone wants to harm you. You feel anxious because you believe you are facing impending doom. You feel peace because you believe all things will work out for good.[30] You feel excited because you believe you are facing impending goodness.

Feelings are the gateway to the emotional realm. Measured over a period of time, your moods and emotions characterize your general personality. A frame of reference filled with conclusions of evil, false and harmful things makes one fearful. A frame of reference filled with good, true and beneficial things makes one peaceful. That is one of the reasons the Bible instructs you to think on what is good and true.[31]

Emotions are neither good nor bad; they are just a response to what you believe. Rather than control an emotion, you should concentrate on managing your beliefs. For instance, you can stifle a "bad emotion" such as anger or fear by suppressing it but that only serves to keep it from being expressed. If you do not want to be angry or fearful, you must challenge the belief that is causing that emotional response.

The primary emotion of a traumatized child is confusion. His mind cannot resolve the event with what he believes to be true so he suppresses it or labels it as an "I can't know" thing. When this condition persists into adulthood it can manifest as a general feeling of confusion.

Any emotional response can be helpful for understanding your personal frame of reference. If you have an emotional response to a situation that seems out of character for you it indicates a false belief or a stronghold. These triggered responses are very valuable for inner healing.

The way you act, or react, is also a result of what you believe. Every action is a response to a conclusion entrenched in your frame of reference.

Addictive behavior originates from beliefs and emotions. That is why strong will power alone will not overcome addiction. Even if you change your behavior in one area, the addiction response will surface in another.

For instance, I know a man that quit smoking cigarettes by transferring his addiction to extreme exercise. While this is considered a healthy option, it did not resolve his inner conflict. He believed he was incapable. He pushed himself in every area of life toward superior performance, but no results could override his frame of reference. His addictions are coping strategies because of that belief.

Your identity is demonstrated by how you act in any given situation, and how you react in specific situations. Actions are what make your character, or personality, obvious to others.

This is the complete chart that depicts the saying: "You are what you believe."

Your identity is who you are being which is expressed by your behavior and emotions. Both of these arise from what you believe to be true. Your beliefs have staying power because they are your frame of reference. Your mind filters all incoming data to resolve conflicts and determine what is good and evil. The reason you experience conflict in this process is because God did not design you to take on *that* responsibility.

Everyone needs to be saved, healed, and reconciled because sin has set a self-referential standard for good and evil. In other words, you are programmed by the sin of pride to determine whether something is good or bad based on how you believe it will affect you. When you determine something to be good, you mean it is good for you. When you determine something is bad, you mean it is bad for you. This sin of pride has separated you from God and marred your ability to reflect His character of love.

Inner Healing

> *... You have put off the old self with its practices and have put on the new self, which is being renewed in knowledge after the image of its Creator.* - *Colossians 3:9-10*

The short definition of inner healing is to reconcile a person's active identity with his or her true identity, or identity in Christ. When we are being someone different than God created us to be there is conflict, and where there is conflict there is pain. We can follow the pain to discover the discrepancy in our identity.

Very often the conclusions we hold about our identity began when we were young, without a great deal of experience or wisdom through which to vet them. These conclusions became ingrained as our personality when new ideas and information were used to confirm preexisting conclusions.

For example, Sean was a colicky baby when he was born. His mom was physically and emotionally fragile, and his dad was a traveling salesman. He was left to cry himself to sleep most of the time, and never felt comforted by his mom. His conclusion: "I'm not loved. I must be unlovable."

For the next fifty years, Sean interpreted every harsh word, skeptical look, and incidence of rejection as proof that he was unlovable. He was plagued with insecurities, addictions, and dysfunctional relationships.

His frame of reference needed to be healed or all his future conclusions would continue in this same pattern. He grew up in the church and memorized Bible verses that spoke of God's love for him, and he believed it to be true in his head. Sadly, his heart did not believe. Trusted advisors and friends told him that he was lovable and offered proof that he was loved.

He nodded ascent with his head, but it made no change to his frame of reference.

He needed inner healing. Somehow he needed a new frame of reference, a new paradigm, a new way of thinking.

Mind Renewal

Do not be conformed to this world, but be transformed by the renewal of your mind ... - Romans 12:2

Sean came for prayer because of another spat with his wife. Something she had said or done triggered the feeling of rejection, and he was driven back to that conclusion of being unlovable.

We prayed for guidance and the Holy Spirit reminded Sean of those early times of feeling unwanted and unloved. I asked him what he believed to be true about himself at that time.

"That I was a bother. That my mom didn't really want me, and that she didn't love me." He paused, and then continued, "I thought there must be something really wrong with me that my own mother didn't love me. I must be completely unlovable."

I asked God to reveal truth to Sean about his identity. He was very quiet for a time, and then I saw him visually relax. He opened his eyes and shared what God had told him.

"God just said: 'You are My son! I love you, and will never let you go.'" He emphasized "My son."

I asked him what that meant to him. He spoke from his heart about the love he felt from God. For the first time his head and heart were in agreement. God had spoken to him in a way that no one else could. The words went right past his mind, and paradigm, and found their mark in his heart.

As we talked about this new truth, Sean began to see how his paradigm distorted earlier messages of being loved. God had shown him that before, but he only accepted it as head-knowledge. His wife had loved him, but he did not feel it, so he rationalized it away. Now he was seeing through a new frame of reference and there was a great deal of evidence that he was lovable.

Inner healing needs to be guided by the Holy Spirit, because a paradigm is such an elusive thing to understand. We do not question things that we have accepted as true because they seem normal. In fact, they are normal to us.

For instance, a common paradigm problem is what we call an *orphan mentality*. This is a frame of reference that can affect anyone, whether they have physically been orphaned or not. An orphan believes that he must protect and provide for himself because no one else will do it for him.

I remember asking a man if he thought he had an orphan mentality. His answer was: "No more than normal." This reminded me to ask God to reveal the answer instead.

Interrogate Beliefs

Our sin nature contributes to the problem of identifying the beliefs of our paradigm. Man hides from God because of his shameful condition, as if avoiding detection will also avoid judgment. Our false beliefs are sinful, so they invoke hiding strategies as well. In shame we attempt to hide our conclusions from others, and for the same reason we even attempt to hide them from ourselves.

| I FEEL | I BELIEVE |

We can identify a belief by carefully considering the way we feel. Some emotions are pleasant and others unpleasant, but they are neither good nor bad. They are responses to what we believe to be true. We cannot control how we feel, but we can interrogate what we believe.

Do you feel an unpleasant emotion, such as sadness, rejection, shame, anger, grief, resentment, hopelessness, fear, rage, envy, insecurity, confusion, pride or guilt? Is it normal for you to feel that way or are you triggered by a particular event, thought or person?

These are the kinds of questions we ask to identify or clarify an emotion. For some people this part is easy because they express their feelings readily and are in touch with their emotions. For others this is very difficult because it has been unwise or unsafe to express them, and they may have suppressed their feelings to the point of not being in touch with their emotions.

The next step is to ask God to reveal what you must believe to be true to make you feel this way. When He gives you the answer, you can take that thought captive to make it obedient to Christ. You make the thought obedient to Christ by confessing the belief and asking God to reveal His truth.

Here is a simple prayer to interrogate beliefs through emotions.

> *Dear Lord, I confess feeling this emotion _____,*
> *Please show me what I believe to be true that causes me*
> *to feel this way.*

When He has revealed the belief continue:

> *I confess that I believe _____ to be true about*
> *me. Please show me how I came to believe this.*

After He has revealed how you came to that conclusion you may need to ask for forgiveness or forgive someone else. Then continue:

> *Now that You have called this to my mind, I am willing to*
> *receive Your truth in its place. Show me the truth about*
> *myself, Lord.*

When God reveals truth it replaces the false belief and resolves any conflict. You are able to live in that truth, and be transformed by it.

We can also identify a belief by considering the way we act. Paul writes in Romans 7 about the conflict between actions and desires. He poses the question: "Why do I do that?" We can get to an underlying belief by working backward from our behavior.

| I ACT > | I BELIEVE |

Do you act in an unpleasant way, such as an addictive habit, a pervasive sin, outbursts of anger, compulsiveness, hiding, isolation, sarcasm or lying? Do you normally act this way or were you triggered by a particular event, thought or person?

These are the kind of questions we ask to identify or clarify aberrant behavior. The challenge for some people is to take a close look at the action, because the hiding strategy is to rationalize or justify the action. The first requirement for successful interrogation of actions is a willingness to be honest.

The next step is to ask God to reveal what you must believe to be true to make you act this way. When He gives you the answer, you can take that thought captive to make it obedient to Christ. Confess the belief and ask God to reveal His truth.

Here is a simple prayer to interrogate beliefs through actions, which is very similar to the prayer for emotions:

Dear Lord, I confess that I act out in this way _____, Please show me what I believe to be true that causes me to act this way.

When He has revealed the belief continue:

I confess that I believe _____ to be true about me. Please show me how I came to believe this.

After He has revealed how you came to that conclusion you may need to ask for forgiveness or forgive someone else. Then continue:

Now that You have called this to my mind, I am willing to receive Your truth in its place. Show me the truth about myself, Lord.

When God reveals truth it replaces the false belief and resolves any conflict. You are able to live in that truth, and be transformed by it.

Persistence of Identity

> *Therefore, if anyone is in Christ, he is a new creation. The old has passed away; behold, the new has come.* - *2 Corinthians 5:17*

God is who He says He is, and you are who God says you are. This is the only accurate assessment of identity, because God is the only accurate judge and He looks at the heart. All His words are true.

If anyone is in Christ, or is living in their identity in Christ, he is a new creation. The old identity has passed away and the new one has come.[32] Healing prayer and mind renewal help a person gain a clear understanding of his or her identity, as God declares it, and they are made into a new person.

We use the term "persistence of identity" to explain how the old nature, or old identity, attempts to hang on or persist. Human nature is resistant to change and tries to find a comfortable pattern, even when it involves pain. When a person takes their identity cues from their past, or from their surroundings, they are held in place and the new personality is blocked.

> *For I do not do the good I want, but the evil I do not want is what I keep on doing.* - *Romans 7:19*

The first challenge with persistence of identity comes from within the person. For some reason they are unable to accept the truth of their healing. It can be a lack of faith, or understanding, or it could be susceptibility to accusation or temptation. They are not able to "hold the territory" and slip back into their old ways of acting and thinking. They revert to their old identity.

For example, a man came for prayer to deal with sexual addiction. He was ashamed of his behavior and tried to manage it with strong willpower. He would build resolve and see success in managing his actions, until something triggered a relapse. Immediately he would be overcome with guilt and shame, and feel like a failure. After some time he would rebuild his resolve and try again, and so the cycle continued. Recovery groups helped him feel stronger, but also made the shame worse when he failed.

When we prayed together, God brought to his memory a specific time when he engaged in sexual sin. He asked God to forgive him for the offense of all his sexual sins, which this specific event represented, and immediately felt a heart change. "God just cleaned me up," he said. He was a free man, and had a new identity. He was full of hope and courage.

A few months later we met again. He felt terrible to admit that he'd relapsed into his addiction. I asked him what had happened to that new cleaned up man that had been forgiven. The enemy of God had accused him of all the other incidents of his sexual addiction, and deceived him into believing he was still in captivity to it. In a moment of weakness he acted in that old way, and then he was accused of having never changed.

We prayed again for forgiveness, and that God would give him a fresh start, and he has been free ever since.

The challenge with an old identity is that it used to fit so well. We can remember the historical accuracy of being that sinner, and then put that persona back on. We can doubt the completeness of our healing and assume there is something else we need to do to keep the new heart. We can be tempted into sin and believe that our identity has changed back because of it.

When God transforms us, He gives us a new heart. We have to accept that new personality in our heart, not just in our head. If we try to hold the territory by brain power instead of faith power, we are at risk of being deceived again.

"Is that all there is to it?"

This is one of our favorite comments from a person that has just received healing in their identity. They have believed a lie for many years, which has been acting as if it is true to them. They believe they are a pervert, or shameful, or worthless, or helpless. God tells them who they really are, and it changes their heart. In amazement they remark: "Really? It's that easy?"

Yes, it is that easy for God. God has given you new life, don't hold on to the old identity. It has no purpose for you, and has been completely redeemed. You are who God says you are.

Do not judge by appearances, but judge with right judgment." - John 7:24

Another form of persistence of identity comes from others around the person. This is the case when a family or group of friends is unwilling to accept the new identity in the person, and holds him accountable to the old identity. It can be a lack of faith or understanding, or it could be fear that the new identity will upset the normal flow of relationship. In the worst cases, they demand that the person reengage the previous identity.

One of our most common examples of this is when one person comes for healing prayer because of an abusive home or family dynamic. When they have received healing and begin living in their new identity, others become agitated. All the normal ways of manipulation and control are no longer effective. The rules of engagement have changed, and the healed one is free from the coercion of others. To restore "order" they insist on each person maintaining his or her original role.

The best case scenario in these situations is that the group or family all receive healing so there is no need for unhealthy ways of relating. When that doesn't happen it can be advisable for the renewed person to separate from the group for a time to avoid the regressive influence. In any case, the new person must learn new ways to relate to the others.

Another example of persistence of identity is because of unforgiveness, which is a major barrier to reconciliation. When a sinner is forgiven by God, they are a new creation. However, if another person holds him accountable for his sin that person is unable to see him in that light. They still view him according to his sin nature.

For instance, a married man committed adultery, which is an egregious offense against his wife and family. He felt conviction from the Holy Spirit and confessed his sin. God forgave him, set him free from that former way of life, and gave him a new identity. However, his wife still held the offense against him and denied that God had forgiven him. She could only see him as the sinful man he had been.

When we teach about reconciliation we use this quotable saying: "God has forgiven me, and He sees me as a new creation. Please agree with Him."

It is characteristic of a loving relationship that each person allows the other to live according to their identity in Christ. No one can remain in authentic relationship with those who demand they live in a false identity. Persistence of identity happens because they are unwilling to accept the new person.

You are who God says you are. Since you are in Christ, you are a new creation. The old has passed away and the new has come. God speaks this truth into your heart and you are changed from the inside out. Your mind accepts the truth from your spirit, and your actions begin to show it. You are free to be the person God created you to be. God has healed and forgiven you, and in His sight you are made righteous. You are perfectly acceptable to God.

You are not who you used to be. This is the important truth you must embrace to avoid persistence of identity from within. The enemy of God will accuse you of past sins, deceive you about the effectiveness of forgiveness, and attempt to destroy God's new creation within you. Stand on the truth. God's word is truth. Receive your new identity in your heart and rehearse it into your mind. You are who God says you are.

You are not who others say you are. This is the important truth you must embrace to avoid being trapped into persistence of identity by others. They may not agree with God's assessment that you have been renewed, but their opinion does not affect your identity. They may be trapped in their own fallen nature and unable to accept your freedom. Intercede on their behalf, asking God to forgive them. Do spiritual warfare from your position of strength. You are able to stand firm because you are who God says you are.

God is the only accurate judge of your identity because He knows the condition of your heart. He can change your hard and sinful heart of stone with His love and mercy.[33] He gives you a new heart, a new personality, a new identity, and a fresh start. The change is immediate and permanent because you are who God say you are, and all His words are true.

Chapter Seven:
Physical Realm

Father, I desire that they also, whom You have given Me, may be with Me where I am, to see My glory that You have given Me because You loved Me before the foundation of the world. - John 17:24

The will of God is that we be united with Him in glory, but in this High Priestly prayer we feel dynamic tension. Jesus does not ask that we be taken out of the world, but protected while we remain in the world. This describes the "already and not yet" aspect of our unification with Him.

Nothing can thwart His ultimate goal. In fact, He promises to use all things to accomplish this goal, even things of evil intent, because we are in agreement with His will (Romans 8:28 paraphrased). We suffer with Christ because the world was subjected to futility by sin,[34] and we will die so that we can be raised again with Him.[35]

Physical healing takes on a new meaning in this light. We should not pray to eliminate suffering on behalf of Christ, though suffering caused by sin has no benefit at all.[36] We should not pray to eliminate physical death since this is part of God's ultimate goal. We should always pray that God redeem our life and convert our suffering to conform to His will.

Hezekiah is a "great" bad example of the power of healing prayer.[37] King Hezekiah became sick and Isaiah the prophet told him that he would not recover. The king prayed for healing. He appealed to God because of his good deeds, and he moved God to compassion by weeping bitterly. God changed His mind(!) and extended Hezekiah's life for fifteen years. A cake of figs was placed on his boil, and he recovered.

Notice that Hezekiah's prayer represented a battle of wills. God had determined that it was time for him to die and be set free from sin, but Hezekiah vehemently disagreed. God did not capitulate to Hezekiah's will but allowed him to have meaningful participation in the timing. Notice also that God used a disease so Hezekiah would die from "natural causes" and a physical remedy to cure the disease. The treatment would not have been effective if God had not changed His mind.

Contrast this attitude with that of the Apostle Paul:

> *For to me to live is Christ, and to die is gain. If I am to live in the flesh, that means fruitful labor for me. Yet which I shall choose I cannot tell. I am hard pressed between the two. My desire is to depart and be with Christ, for that is far better. But to remain in the flesh is more necessary on your account.* - *Philippians 1:21-24*

Paul was not depressed or suicidal. His desire was to *depart and be with Christ*. He was not motivated by fear of pain in his suffering but by his invitation to full relationship with Christ. He described the tension between life and ministry on earth, which includes suffering, compared to life and ministry in heaven, which is filled with glory. This was not an either / or question for him but one of timing.

We pray differently for physical healing when we operate from a place of spiritual and emotional wholeness. We are motivated by God's perfect will because we know it will be accomplished. At the same time we are motivated by God's good will because we know He turns all things to serve His purpose. In wholeness, God's perfect will is also our purpose.

Expect physical healing to accompany spiritual and emotional healing because God brings wholeness to the person in each realm. The order in which healing manifests is up to God. Jesus demonstrated this in His ministry when He healed some in the spiritual realm first and others in the physical.

For example, of the ten lepers that were healed, only the Samaritan leper returned to thank Jesus.

> *When He saw them He said to them, "Go and show yourselves to the priests." And as they went they were*

cleansed. Then one of them, when he saw that he was healed, turned back, praising God with a loud voice; and he fell on his face at Jesus' feet, giving Him thanks. Now he was a Samaritan. - Luke 17:14-16

This leper was first healed physically, then emotionally and spiritually. He was physically healed *as he went* and the manifestation came with that obedient step of faith. Then he was emotionally healed as manifested by *praising God with a loud voice*. Finally, He was reconciled to God and spiritually healed as demonstrated by his humble act of worship and thanksgiving.

In this example the recorded sequence happens so quickly the steps of progression are hard to distinguish. I exaggerated the sequence in my paraphrase to help our Western mindset follow the steps. Hebrew culture, however, is more comfortable with the "prophetic tense" in which the "truth" is more important than the "method." In other words, reporting "what happened" is more important than "how it happened."

Whether healing manifests quickly or slowly between the realms, we know by faith that it is as good as done in a prophetic sense. When the presenting symptom is physical, that is a good place to start the healing process, but if healing begins in the spiritual or emotional realms we can expect wholeness to manifest in the physical as well.

Signs and Wonders

Now many signs and wonders were regularly done among the people by the hands of the apostles. ... And more than ever believers were added to the Lord. ... The people also gathered from the towns around Jerusalem, bringing the sick and those afflicted with unclean spirits, and they were all healed. - Acts 5:12-16

I love to pray for physical healing because it is dramatic and the effect is obvious to the person being healed and everyone that witnesses it. Spiritual healing reconciles a person to God in the unseen realm. Emotional healing renews his mind, but that is also the unseen realm. Physical healing is tangible, verifiable, and demonstrable.

People flocked to Jesus everywhere He went because of signs and wonders, including physical healing. He used their curiosity and intrigue as an opening to teach about the plan of salvation and the way to be reconciled to God.[38] The physical healing was never His only goal but served as a starting point for complete healing and reconciliation with God.[39]

Jesus promised that His followers would do the signs and wonders that He did, and even greater works (John 14:12). He proclaimed that signs and wonders would accompany believers (Mark 16:17). He explained that the power to do these works would come through the Holy Spirit.[40] When we witness blind people given sight, lame people walking, paralyzed people moving, sick people getting better, and the dead being raised, these are signs that His authority over sickness and disease has been transferred to us through Pentecost. We can expect God to heal in answer to our prayers because we believe and follow Him.

One afternoon, my friend Bill Timm and I prayed for Sam, a man that had walked with a limp for nearly forty years. In a short conversation we learned that he had accepted Jesus as his Savior a few years before and was trying to live a Christian life. As we began praying with him, I sensed that he was not sure of his salvation. He was forcing himself to believe, but doubted from time to time.

"God loves you, and would like you to be well," Bill told him. "We would like to pray for your healing."

Sam sat in a chair, Bill knelt at his feet, and I laid my hands on his shoulders. Bill commanded his left leg to grow until it was the same length as his right leg. As we watched, his leg grew about an inch and a half. It took less than a minute.

"I can feel it growing!" Sam exclaimed. "I can feel something is happening inside of me."

"Do you know that God loves you?" I asked.

"I know it! I know it now. I know it!" Sam said exuberantly. He stood up and tested his balance, twisted back and forth a few times, and then took a few steps. God had reassured him that he was really loved, and then He demonstrated it in his body.

There were times when Jesus did a miracle to demonstrate His authority. He healed the man with a withered hand to prove to the Pharisees that it was God's will to heal on the Sabbath.[41] He healed the paralytic to prove to them that He had the authority to forgive sins.[42] He raised Lazarus from the dead to prove that He had conquered death.[43]

Wayne agreed to meet with me for prayer on the advice of his pastor because of broken relationships in his life. As far back as he could remember, he could not get along with people. There were some pervasive issues standing in the way of his wholeness, and we began to pray for guidance.

During our prayer time Wayne showed signs of distress. He had been fighting a headache all day, and it was getting worse. A few minutes later he asked if we could schedule another prayer time because the pain was so intense.

"Heavenly Father, I ask You to heal Wayne's headache right now!" I prayed with authority.

"Wow!" Wayne exclaimed. "The pain just disappeared. It's completely gone!"

This was a situation in which the enemy attempted to derail the prayer time. I knew we had been making progress, and had every confidence that God wanted to complete the work in the spiritual realm. When God healed Wayne's headache, it opened the way for healing in his spirit.

As you can imagine, his faith was significantly increased from the experience. Because God touched his physical realm, Wayne was willing to trust God in his emotional and spiritual realms too.

Pray for healing in the physical realm because our Heavenly Father is supernatural. He can make supernatural changes because He is the Creator of law and order, and He alone can override them for His good purposes.

The Ways of the Lord

> *"And because you listen to these rules and keep and do them, the LORD your God will keep with you the covenant and the steadfast love that He swore to your fathers. He will love you, bless you, and multiply you. ... And the LORD will take away from you all sickness, and none of the evil diseases of Egypt, which you knew, will He inflict on you, but He will lay them on all who hate you. - Deuteronomy 7:12-15*

Moses described the ways of the Lord in the Pentateuch. The book of Deuteronomy is particularly loaded with cautions and explanations about the things that lead to blessings compared to those that lead to curses. When we listen to His rules and obey them we will be blessed. If we ignore His rules and turn to other gods we will be cursed. There is a very clear correlation.

The lesson we learn from Job's friends is that we are not to judge. The lesson we learn from the disciples asking about the sin that caused the man to be born blind is the same: do not judge. Sometimes people interpret from these lessons that there is no connection between sin and disease or other consequences. But that is not an accurate understanding. For example, Jesus told the recently healed paralytic not to go on sinning or something worse might happen to him.[44]

I do not think that God's commands, laws, statutes and covenant are to be treated as the rules for a lifelong test by which our righteousness will be measured. We have already failed that test. Rather, these instructions should be understood as God's explanation of the way things work.

We can expect divine health because of these rights and promises. Divine health is a condition in which we are protected by God's hand. No matter what happens around us, we know that He is our peace, our *shalom*.

For instance, God protected the Israelites as they traveled through the wilderness so they did not get sick, nor did their shoes wear out.[45] Yet some rebelled and died from fire, plagues, vipers or earthquake. God protected the prophets from famine, pestilence, and war. Yet Elisha died from an illness (2 Kings 13:14). Divine health does not circumvent death, but protects us for powerful living until the time God has ordained[46].

When I pray for physical healing, I listen for the Lord to reveal any place where the person is disobeying or resisting His *way*. The Holy Spirit convicts of sin, and sometimes the symptoms of sin are obvious. After all, the purpose of pain is to show where we are out of sync with God. When we confess our sin He is willing to forgive us our sin and cleanse us from all unrighteousness.[47]

Let me share a personal example. My wife and I have the privilege of spending a week or so in Mesa, Arizona during the winter, visiting with her mother. It is a nice setting to relax, catch up on reading and conversation, and soak up some sunshine before heading back to our home in the Pacific Northwest.

A few years ago I got quite sick while we were there. I wondered if it was food poisoning from a restaurant, but it persisted for several days like the flu. We prayed for healing.

I was beginning to improve on the third day, and then I recognized a pattern. This year it was the flu, but the year before I had a miserable cold, and the year before that I had missed a few days as well. I inquired of God about this issue. I wondered why He would allow the enemy to rob me of vacation days.

He reminded me of His commandment: "Remember the Sabbath day to keep it holy.[48]" Immediately I considered my standard weekly calendar and noticed that there was insufficient time for rest and restoration. I was out of balance with the Designer's specifications. My choices gave the enemy permission to afflict me.

105

I repented of my sin and made changes in my schedule to protect times of Sabbath rest. He allowed me to regain strength at a natural pace that year, but I have not fallen back into that pattern since. God's ways are right and true, and He shares them with us in His word.[49]

Praise the Lord that He forgives and cleanses us from all unrighteousness.

> And I heard a loud voice in heaven, saying, "Now the salvation and the power and the kingdom of our God and the authority of His Christ have come, for the accuser of our brothers has been thrown down, who accuses them day and night before our God. And they have conquered him by the blood of the Lamb and by the word of their testimony, for they loved not their lives even unto death. - Revelation 12:10-11

The accuser of the brethren is the devil. Notice that he accuses us day and night. He is a deceiver, and the father of lies. One of the things he wants us to believe is that we are condemned to die because of our sin. He is insanely jealous of our relationship with God and will use any deception to rob us of our spiritual inheritance.

If you are an adopted son of God, then you have access to all the power and authority that Jesus did as the Son of Man. Your rights include divine health, power over unclean spirits, ability to cure diseases, and heal sicknesses.[50]

But the devil wants us to live in fear and abdicate our authority. He feeds a constant stream of lies to destroy faith and wisdom. He would have us believe there is no remedy for sin. He tempts us to take matters into our own hands, thereby limiting our power to that of a fallen human. Like Job's wife, he is inciting you to "curse God and die.[51]"

The saints have conquered him by the blood of the Lamb, which is a reference to the power of forgiveness, and the word of their testimony, which is a reference to their faith. They were victorious because they loved God, even more than their own lives.

Jesus told the unsure father of a demon possessed boy that all things are possible for one who believes.[52] The devil accuses us of being disqualified, and that, for some reason, God's promises do not apply to us.

It is a fight for faith. We are not fighting against God, or His will, but against the enemy in the spiritual realm who is trying to deny us from receiving all God has for us. Pray boldly for physical healing and wholeness in your relationship with God. Do not let unbelief or deception stand in the way of the great gifts God has in mind for you.

Your Highest Authority

> *Take care, brothers, lest there be in any of you an evil, unbelieving heart, leading you to fall away from the living God. - Hebrews 3:12*

What you hold as your highest authority determines the maximum power you are able to access. If your authority is not up to the task you are subject to its limitations. This is profoundly obvious in the physical realm.

In the mid-seventies, my father-in-law, Victor, had a bad case of the flu, and shortly after began having chronic pain. At first he tried to manage it with over the counter drugs, rest, soup, and other home remedies. He was being the highest authority over his body.

After several weeks of pain he went to see his family doctor. This doctor had more medical education and experience than my father-in-law, and was accepted as the higher authority. Victor took his doctor's advice with great confidence, but the pain persisted. Finally, his doctor told him there was nothing more he could do except to refer him to a specialist.

Vic's symptoms were diagnosed as rheumatoid arthritis, and he was referred from one specialist to another. He had great confidence in each new doctor and his or her expertise until the Mayo Clinic gave him the news there was nothing more they could do for him. They could manage his pain, but could not offer a cure. He had the greatest respect for them and was very disappointed that they were out of ideas. His highest hopes were limited by traditional education and experience.

Next he turned to alternative medicine on the hopes that greater power might be available through practitioners that were unconstrained by government oversight. Loving family members and friends made all kinds of recommendations, from the traditional to the absurd. Each of these "new" authorities failed in turn.

His health continued to decline, and the side effects of the treatments compromised his body, compounding the problems. He explored avenues that would have never before crossed his mind. Well-meaning friends gave him information on experimental drugs, hidden formulas, faith healers and mystics.

He accepted the Lord as his Savior just a few weeks before he died. Though his body was wasting away, his inner self became renewed that day, and his healing was complete. He had placed his trust in the Highest Authority who would never say "there is nothing more I can do for you." Instead, God said, "Vic, you may enter My rest.[53]"

The Greek worldview overvalues knowledge and relies on education and experience to determine authority. This is particularly dangerous when coupled with mankind's loss of identity. A person desperately trying to discover who he is may regard a representative of science as his highest authority.

For example, when a person feels pain he goes to a clinic or hospital for evaluation. The protocol is to collect facts about him, including a list of symptoms. A chart or database is consulted to match the presenting group of symptoms with a disease or condition known to cause them. These results are tested for consistency and lead to a diagnosis and prognosis. A label or name is given to the condition, and the patient is treated accordingly. The patient, desperate for an identity, accepts the label as the definition of who he is.

"You are clinically depressed," declares the specialist.

"Oh, thank you doctor!" he says. "This explains everything about me."

Unfortunately, it also "explains" everything about the patient's future. The charts prophetically call forth the development of the disease or condition until it finds its completion in death. The patient's limitations are catalogued and his decline is predicted based on the experiences of others. It is an identity, though not a good one.

A similarly frightening scenario happens when a person is looking for an identity and the test results are inconclusive. An undiagnosed pain sends her from one authority to another until she finds one willing to confer an identity on her.

Here is a list of some mystery illnesses, or conditions that are hard to diagnose: Irritable bowel syndrome (IBS), Celiac disease, fibromyalgia, rheumatoid arthritis, multiple sclerosis (MS), Lyme disease, lupus, polycystic ovary syndrome (PCOS), endometriosis, migraines, hypothyroidism, diabetes, Crohn's disease, colitis, bipolar disorder and other psychological and emotional conditions.

I believe the devil uses these illnesses and other conditions in a nasty scheme to con people into false identities. He tempts them through pain and fear so they scurry to find relief. If they do not have God as their highest authority they are susceptible to any number of lies and misinterpretations. He robs them of their true identities by offering explanations (excuses) for their active identities.

The person that does not know his identity in Christ and does not hold God as his highest authority is vulnerable to these temptations. Rather than be transformed by the renewing of his mind, he will accept the label offered by some other authority as an identity and use that as a guide for his life.

For this reason, whenever there is an undiagnosed pain or symptoms are hard to diagnose I begin by assuming it is a spiritual attack. Many times I have seen these symptoms disappear as soon as we take authority over an oppressive spirit of fear or other interloper.

However, the person that accepts the Lord God as his highest authority will never hear a declaration of "this is who you are, and there is nothing more we can do for you." He is free to discover his identity in Christ, and overcome the wiles of the devil.

The Lord is our Healer.

Chapter Eight:
Complete Healing

My peace I give to you. - John 14:27

Randy was a young man that grew up in a Christian home with loving parents, but he was insecure, often sick, and unsure of his identity. He came to ask God to reveal the calling on his life. I asked about his passions, desires, pains and frustrations to build a framework from which to pray. He talked about his heart for evangelism and helping others, and then described his physical constraints.

"I get started on something, but it seems like I get sick at just the wrong time. It's was very hard for me to finish school because of it, and it took a long time. I've always been weak, and I come down with anything that's going around," he said.

I taught him about the power of word curses, and how the words he spoke compromised his health. He quickly understood and repented. Then I asked him if he knew the cause of his health issues.

"We haven't figured that out yet," he answered. "It's hard to diagnose."

Then he recited a long list of symptoms that he has, and shared some ideas of what the offending condition might be.

"You've given a lot of thought to symptoms of disease. Can you tell me how you would know if you were healthy?" I asked.

He paused for quite a while on that question. He had not thought much about symptoms of health. This led to a great conversation about knowing your strength instead of focusing on your weakness. We brainstormed some symptoms of health, such as the ability to run a certain distance, memorize scripture, relate to strangers, and the like.

Over the next several minutes we broke off word curses, dealt with a spirit of fear, and he repented of settling for a weak identity. He was excited to try out his new way of thinking, and had selected several symptoms through which he could test his health. Instead of absorbing energy he began to exude it, and that was a sign of life to me.

Praise the Lord!

Complete healing is a process that occurs as you accept God's conversion plan for your life and exchange your active identity for your true identity in Christ. The Holy Spirit guides the process of reconciliation until anything that is out of balance conforms to the Truth.

Reconciled to God

> *You keep him in perfect peace whose mind is stayed on You, because he trusts in You.* - Isaiah 26:3

Isaiah prophesied perfect peace over anyone who trusts God and whose mind is stayed on Him.

When have you felt God's perfect peace?

I call this the sweet spot. It is the condition of *shalom*, and it is a gift that must be stewarded. The first experience usually comes at salvation. That moment of surrender leads to an awareness of God's love and then the Holy Spirit enters as the Father's deposit that guarantees the inheritance to come.

The deposit grows as we learn to submit to the Holy Spirit and walk in His ways and become Spirit filled. Some are filled suddenly, as the disciples were on Pentecost. Their heart is ready to receive the Holy Spirit and their soul makes no argument. Others are filled slowly, as if by a garden hose, rather than immersion. Their heart is ready to receive the Holy Spirit but their soul surrenders reluctantly.

Whether your experience has been sudden or slow, you must care for the gift of the Spirit by which you are reconciled to God. Spend time in prayer and worship on a regular basis so you can tune out the noise of self and the world. Practice the presence of God so you can hear Him through your soul, your mind, will and emotions.

Karl came for prayer because of heart disease, though he was a little skeptical about treating his physical condition with prayer. He had been saved a few years before and had settled into church life, but did not expect much more from God.

"I pray, but I don't ask God for much," he told me. "I mostly pray for the big stuff, like when I really need help."

It was not a surprise to me that the first place God took us in prayer was Karl's inability to be loved. He had been rejected and vowed never to be dependent on anyone again. I helped him break off that rash vow and he received a blessing of love in its place.

"Do you feel any different?" I asked.

His eyes moved side to side and he fidgeted a little as he tested, then replied: "Not much. Maybe just a little warmth in my chest."

"Can you point to the spot?" I sensed in the Spirit where it was, and Karl put his finger right on the spot to confirm.

"Is it about the size of a dime?" He nodded, and I continued: "Pay attention to that spot as it grows."

His eyes widened, so on that cue I asked: "Is it about the size of a half dollar now?"

He nodded. A relatively short sequence followed: the size of a cup, quart, a gallon?

"You know how big a washtub is?" he interrupted in his southern drawl. "It's gone that big!"

This is an example of how to steward the presence of the Holy Spirit. Karl needed some help to recognize the feeling of peace, and then some coaching to allow it to expand. You may recognize the peace as you pray. If not, recall the feeling from a previous time, such as a retreat, worship service, prayer session, or by going all the way back to your salvation experience. Pay attention to the sense of peace and invite the Holy Spirit to increase His presence. He will.

This is the process of being reconciled to God. The Holy Spirit will grow inside until He reaches a barrier, such as an unconfessed sin or stronghold. These obstacles are taken away when you surrender your rights to yourself and ask for pardon in the areas where you have separated yourself from God. The Spirit of God will fill that space. Continue in this way until He has filled every part of you.

> *Behold, I have given you authority to tread on serpents and scorpions, and over all the power of the enemy, and nothing shall hurt you. Nevertheless, do not rejoice in this, that the spirits are subject to you, but rejoice that your names are written in heaven." - Luke 10:19-20*

The person that is reconciled to God has become inhospitable territory for the enemy. Demons, unclean spirits, curses and other schemes of the devil are not welcome in the presence of God. The Spirit inside is the authority you need over all the power of the enemy.

Jesus told the disciples to rejoice that their names are written in heaven. Having our names written in heaven means we are in complete, perfect, and eternal unity with the Father, Son and Holy Spirit, just as Jesus prayed in John 17. The ultimate outcome of this unity is heaven, and the immediate outcome is authority and power to do His will.

> *And the peace of God, which surpasses all understanding, will guard your hearts and your minds in Christ Jesus. - Philippians 4:7*

Complete healing means to be reconciled to God and to be in perfect relationship with Him. This manifests first in the spiritual realm, and then ultimately in the emotional and physical realms as well.

Reconciled to Self

For you have died, and your life is hidden with Christ in God. · Colossians 3:3

When Michael first came for prayer it was because his wife of thirty-plus years had filed for a divorce. She would not take any more of his pornography, strip clubs and massage parlors, nor his controlling temper and self-justification. He knew she was right but he lacked the will power to change.

"I've done her wrong," he confessed sadly. "But I don't want to lose her. Do you think there is any chance she'd take me back?"

"Honestly, Michael, I think she's married to the wrong man," I answered. "I wouldn't advise her to take you back." Then I continued: "If you were being the man God created you to be it would be a completely different story."

Michael had been sexually abused when he was young and lived on his own before he turned eighteen. He had developed many harmful coping strategies because of the pain, shame and rejection. He was trapped in an identity that felt responsible to protect that little boy, and no amount of rational thought could free him.

As we prayed together, the Holy Spirit convicted him of his sin and he prayed for forgiveness. He died to that old nature and the change in his personality was astonishing. For the first time in his life he felt authentic connection to his true identity. A few months later he was reconciled to his wife and they renewed their vows. She was finally married to the right man after more than thirty years.

You are who God says you are, and you can only discover your true identity by listening to Him. Identity crises happen when people try to become something of their own making, when they listen to lies about who they are, or when they look for their identity in the wrong places.

Self-Directed

A culture of freedom, independence and liberty contribute greatly to identity crises. The promise that you can be whoever you want to be ignores the truth that you may not be suited to that identity. For instance, I know a man who wanted the prestige, authority and lifestyle of a dentist, and with great effort and sacrifice he achieved his goal. Unfortunately, he hated the career he had earned but would not change it for economic reasons. He suffered conflict and pain as a result of his false identity.

Deception

The sinful nature is built on a false foundation. The devil, a liar[54] and accuser,[55] understands that you act out what you believe. He feeds you a steady diet of lies and accusations to keep you from discovering your true identity. He manipulates with fear, guilt, shame and greed, cloaking your true identity and divine design in the emotional realm.

What do you see when you look in the mirror?

Most people are immediately confronted by problems, flaws, imperfections and sin. It is not hard to find these because the accuser points them out. Those with a Greek worldview (as discussed in Chapter 1) see failure in the physical realm compared to a phantom standard. Those with a Hebrew worldview see failure in the emotional and spiritual realms, such as not belonging or being able to relate. This is hardly the reflection of God in whose image they were created.[56]

Janette could see issues and problems reflected in her mirror and concluded that she was unlovable. She got angry at my wife for saying that she was loved. She could not believe anyone would love her when she did not even love herself. Even though she sang "Jesus loves me, this I know" as a child, she did not believe it personally. She was unlovable, and thought that even God could not love her.

Warren could see issues and problems reflected in his mirror and concluded that he was better off dead. There was no hope for him because his sin was too great to overcome. He believed he was disqualified from any godly purpose because of his faults, and wondered why he was still alive. It felt pointless to him.

Sarah could see issues and problems reflected in her mirror and concluded that she was unacceptable. Even though her dad had never yelled at her, she believed she was just as worthless as her older siblings who were the direct recipients of his tirades. There was no need for him to single her out; she had already jumped to that conclusion.

These are examples of the lies spread by the enemy of God to give His children identity crises. How can a person express his identity in Christ when he believes he is unlovable, unacceptable, or better off dead?

We have to take thoughts like these captive and make them obedient to Christ. We have to interrogate them and receive truth in their place. Healing requires each false identity to be reconciled, or made to conform, to the appropriate identity in Christ. Otherwise people like Michael, Janette, Warren, and Sarah are trapped in their false identity, conflict and pain.

The Wrong Source

Identity confusion also occurs when a person tries to discover his identity through the wrong source. The most persuasive voice he hears comes from the one he considers his highest authority. If God is not the highest authority in his life then he will look to another source for his identity. A label or identity can come from a parent, teacher, boss or professional.

For example, Cynthia was a troubled young woman. She was pretty, outgoing, and popular but nothing satisfied the empty feeling inside. Soon she was abusing drugs and alcohol, living a wild life, and running afoul of the law. People shook their head at her and sighed at the train wreck her life had become. She had no explanation for her feelings, thoughts, or actions.

Finally she was forced by the courts to enter a rehabilitation program. She hoped it would solve her troubles, and give her a clue about her identity. A psychiatric evaluation diagnosed her with bipolar disorder and manic-depressive illness. She was relieved! This explained everything, from the erratic behavior to the uncontrollable emotions.

Cynthia accepted the professionals of the medical community as her highest authority. She embraced this identity because it seemed to resolve the conflict inside. But the real Cynthia was not reconciled to her identity in Christ, and she did not seek God as highest authority. The troubles and poor coping strategies quickly returned and she continued a life of conflict and pain.

Cynthia's situation is not unusual in our culture. People spend a lot of time, money, and energy trying to discover their identity through wrong sources, such as medical science. Imagine what would happen if they spent those resources discovering their identity in Christ instead.

Discover Yourself

For we are His workmanship, created in Christ Jesus for good works, which God prepared beforehand, that we should walk in them. - Ephesians 2:10

When have you felt at peace with yourself?

God created you on purpose and for a purpose. The fact that you are His workmanship means that He drew the blueprint and designed you according to His specifications. The fact that you were created for good works means that you have a calling to perform. Your sweet spot is where your God-given capabilities are used for maximum benefit to perform your God-given good works.

This is your true identity. It is your identity in Christ that fits you perfectly. You are comfortable in your own skin. Your hard work makes you tired, but it is a good tired. Your efforts are rewarded with a thirty, sixty, and hundred fold return.[57] You are free to be yourself because you are perfectly acceptable. You experience *shalom* in every part of your life.

Do not be conformed to this world, but be transformed by the renewal of your mind, that by testing you may discern what is the will of God, what is good and acceptable and perfect. - Romans 12:2

You are transformed from your active identity into your true identity by the renewing of your mind. Since you act and feel according to what you believe, reconciliation requires conforming your beliefs so they are in agreement with what God says. Then your character will reflect God's character.

The work of reconciliation is triggered by pain that comes from conflict between whom you are being and who you were designed to be. Use that pain to identify the beliefs, emotions and behaviors that need to be interrogated. Your transformed identity will conform to God's blueprint, so whenever you are acting "out of character" it is a reminder that more mind renewal is needed.

Complete healing means to be reconciled to your true self.

Reconciled to Others

For just as the body is one and has many members, and all the members of the body, though many, are one body, so it is with Christ. - 1 Corinthians 12:12

Healing happens in community.

We understand who God is through the patterns He displays. For instance, the Trinity model expresses the Godhead as three members in one body. Paul applies this principle to the *church of the heart*[58] by describing it as one body made up of many members.

God's assessment is that nothing is impossible to the body that operates in this way. In the account of the Tower of Babel, God identified that the people were unified, able to communicate freely, had made a plan, and therefore nothing they proposed to do would be impossible for them.[59] In this case they had made a plan of rebellion against God so He used His supernatural power to frustrate their progress. Imagine if the body of Christ were reconciled to that model with a plan that agreed with God. I believe He would use His supernatural power to facilitate its progress.

We, as the body of Christ, are in the process of being healed as we reconcile with one another. Wherever you find a *church of the heart* that emulates this character of God you will also find a place of healing. The Holy Spirit metes out the gifts so they complement each other and the whole body is equipped. When all the members participate there is a perfect mix that is complete, balanced and loving.

Healing happens in this kind of community as one member holds another accountable, yet another encourages, and another brings a word of knowledge. Each acts as witness for the others and the schemes of the enemy are thwarted.

> *If possible, so far as it depends on you, live peaceably with all.* - Romans 12:18

An individual can experience personal healing and wholeness no matter what anyone else chooses, but reconciliation requires agreement by both parties. The first order of business is to deal with your own discrepancies, to forgive and be forgiven until you are at peace with your integrity and identity.

In Paul's letter to the Romans we are instructed to live peaceably (be reconciled) with all *so far as it depends on us.* The limit to reconciliation is determined by the standard to which we are reconciled. In other words, when we are reconciled to God we are not able to be reconciled to the sin nature. That means we cannot be reconciled to the part of a person that is trapped in sin nature.

God is reconciling the world to Himself through Jesus Christ, and if anyone is in Christ (forgiven), he is a new creation. When you are reconciled to God you are also reconciled to anyone that is in Christ.

Complete healing means to be reconciled to the God-nature in others.

Chapter Nine:
Interceding for Others

Truth is lacking, and he who departs from evil makes himself a prey. The LORD saw it, and it displeased Him that there was no justice. He saw that there was no man, and wondered that there was no one to intercede; then His own arm brought him salvation, and His righteousness upheld him. -Isaiah 59:15-16

The verb intercede means to plead on another's behalf, to intervene between parties, or to act as a mediator in a dispute. In the case of intercessory prayer it means to plead for mercy from God on behalf of another who is either unable or unwilling to ask.

Anyone can act as an intercessor and pray for another that they be healed. The only requirements are faith, hope and love. You must have faith in God as the source of power for healing. You must have hope in a blessed future as God has promised. You must love the person (recipient) so you can pray earnestly and effectively.

There are no guarantees that the recipient will receive the truth, because they have a role to play. God will not override their free will, and some will persist in rejecting Him. But the rewards of intercession are supernatural.

Sharing Hope

A person needs healing when he is in pain or bondage because of sin. The inner circle is labeled "lie" because sin causes him to believe something false, and that belief separates him from God. The lie acts as if it is true to him, and results in pain in the spiritual, emotional and physical realms. This lie is inserted into his frame of reference when he misinterprets a life situation, or when he is deceived by someone else. The lie must be overcome by truth.

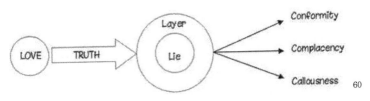

The truth can be blocked by a protective layer. For example, a person that believes he is worthless (the lie) may expend great energy doing things for others (the layer). By expending energy for others he hopes to convince them that he is valuable, even indispensable, but his efforts are really a cover for his feelings of worthlessness. In another example, a person with fear of rejection (the lie) may be horribly obnoxious to others (the layer) in a preemptive strike to reject before being rejected. In a final example, a self-loathing person (the lie) may abuse drugs or alcohol (the layer) to mask the pain of feeling unlovable.

The intercessor is motivated by love to intervene on behalf of the recipient. However, if the truth is directed at the layer instead of the lie it misses the mark and cannot heal the root cause. Depending on his temperament, the one receiving prayer will respond with conformity, complacency, or callousness.

The conformist will hear the truth and readily agree in his mind. He will then apply the truth to the layer and attempt to control it with strong will power. Because the root cause has not received truth, the conformist will ultimately fail in changing the behavior or emotion of the layer. This turns into a cycle of resolve, effort, failure, discouragement leading back to greater resolve, and on it goes. For example, the obnoxious man tries with great effort to be nice but gives up when he still feels rejected. Similarly, the self-loathing man swears off drugs and lives a clean and sober life, until he realizes he still hates himself, at which point he abuses drugs worse than before.

The complacent one will discredit the truth and hunker down with a victim mentality. Since the truth is applied to the layer instead of the root cause, he is unwilling to accept it.

For example, the overachiever ignores the recommendation to find a balance, convinced that creating value is a good thing. Similarly, the self-loathing man continues to justify his drinking. Alcohol is the layer with which he is trying to solve the problem of his pain, which is caused by a lie.

The callous one will respond with rebellion or withdrawal, depending on his fight or flight character. The fight temperament will argue against the truth and actively reject it. The flight temperament will ignore the truth entirely. In either case, he will become more entrenched in his belief (lie) through the searing of his conscience, at which point he will become insensitive to the truth.

Loving Through

The key to intercession is to pray with and for a person without judging them. It is crucial to love them so much that you can see past the layer and into the lie. You must love past their behavior, though it may be repugnant. You must love past their beliefs, even if they are prejudicial and hateful. You must love past their deception, knowing that they may be unaware of it since they are being deceived and deceiving themselves.

The controlling lie is exposed when the person surrenders the layer. This is an act of will on his part. It requires him to be vulnerable.

Love is to know another person, and to be known by him. The intercessor must express this kind of love to the recipient to establish a level of trust that allows him to surrender the layer. In this setting, truth can be delivered directly to the lie instead of being blocked by the layer. Then truth takes the place of the lie and eliminates the root cause of pain in him.

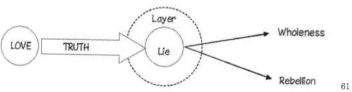

61

There are two possible responses to the truth, wholeness (healing) or rebellion.

Some will reject the truth and resent the intimate intrusion of their privacy. They are the ones who have come face to face with healing and choose to walk away instead. They go away sad, as did the Rich Young Ruler after receiving truth from Jesus.[62] This sears the conscience, causing them to be less sensitive to truth each time they reject it.

Others will accept truth and rejoice greatly at the intimate expression of unconditional love. They receive deep cleansing in their identity and the behaviors and pain of sin no longer has a stronghold. This heals their conscience and prepares them to be more sensitive to truth over time.

Sharing Truth

Here is an intercessor's step by step guide to sharing truth with a recipient in a prayer appointment.

- Discover the pain – pray for guidance to reveal the pain in the spiritual, emotional and physical realms. Trust the Holy Spirit to introduce the starting point.

- Identify the false belief – allow the pain to point to the lie. Note any behavioral or emotional coping layers that emanate from the false belief.

- Pray for revelation of the root – ask God to reveal the source of this belief, that is when he came to believe it to be true.

- Interrogate the belief – have the recipient confirm the false belief and whether it feels true to him.

- Confess and repent – confess the false belief in prayer and ask God to forgive him for believing it to be true.

- Pray for truth – ask God to reveal truth to replace the lie and listen for His revelation.

- Witness and confirm – allow the recipient to share the truth he received from God. Confirm the word of God and agree that it replaces the former belief.

- Test for peace – ask him or her if they have a sense of peace in that area, and confirm their wholeness and healing.

Free Indeed

Therefore, confess your sins to one another and pray for one another, that you may be healed. The prayer of a righteous person has great power as it is working. -James 5:16

When a person receives the truth from God, it is delivered directly into their heart. The truth placed into their heart is received experientially, and becomes true to them.

Healing is expressed in the whole person. In the spiritual realm their freedom is experienced as peace, comfort and closeness to God. In the emotional realm it is experienced as relief, joy, calmness and confidence. In the physical realm it is experienced as a weight being lifted, an ability to breathe, a release of a burden, and lightness.

Wholeness is demonstrated by transformation. In the spiritual realm the recipient will have healed relationships with God and others. In the emotional realm he will be free from fear and able to express happiness. In the physical realm his pains and diseases disappear as strength and vitality return.

The rewards are supernatural. God is connected to the intercessor with unconditional love. The intercessor then connects with the recipient with a heart of love. The truth is delivered through this connection to replace the lie and provide freedom. As a divinely orchestrated byproduct, the intercessor increases in faith, hope and love.

Cautions and Practical Matters

The Holy Spirit guides the prayer appointment in the most effective way. Learn to trust His leading and you will see more praiseworthy results.

The primary role of the intercessor is to help the recipient work through barriers to healing. The first step the intercessor needs to take is to remove barriers that he or she has brought into the prayer appointment.

Judgment Disqualifies

If there is the slightest trace of judgment in your heart toward a person then you are disqualified from interceding for him or her. True intercession is to pray according to the will of God, and it is impossible to agree with God's will when you are holding judgment.

There is a difference between discernment and judgment. The first is an awareness of the sin and its offense to godliness, the second is a desire for the person to be held responsible for that sin. The only way for a person to receive healing is for God to reconcile him, and that comes through forgiveness, which is an act of mercy. The intercessor is in direct conflict with the mercy of God to the extent that he condemns the petitioner for his sin.

I learned this lesson the hard way. Greg used his imposing presence to exercise control over others, including his wife and children. He agreed to meet with me because it was the "right thing to do," but he believed it would not change his wife's behavior. That attitude caused me to anticipate he was extremely self-referential and possibly a narcissist. We met several times for prayer, but each session devolved into opinionated discussion. We made no progress toward truth.

"Lord, why can't we break through these barriers?" I prayed one evening after we had met. "What is going on that holds Greg so tightly?"

"Why are you striving? You've been disqualified." I heard the Lord reply.

I immediately understood. Greg was being the kind of person I detest the most: controlling others with his interpretation of the Bible and subjecting them to spiritual abuse. Deep down I wanted him to suffer for all the pain he caused others. Because of God's words, my heart was broken by conviction.

"Lord, help me see Greg the way You do," I responded.

I began to see Greg's life story in a different light. He had shared about the abuse he suffered as a child and feelings of rejection and betrayal from his parents. He had no role models and adopted his defensive strategy because of his orphan mentality. He hated being hurt and believed he would never treat someone the way he had been treated. Ironically, he could not see the pain he caused others because his frame of reference was so warped.

My heart broke for Greg, and I asked God to forgive me for holding him in my judgment. Though God has forgiven me, Greg has not and the chance to intercede with him has passed. Whenever I think of him it reminds me that "hurt people hurt people."

Keep from judging others by reminding yourself that everyone has a story. If you knew what they had gone through, your heart would be filled with compassion. Allow yourself to pray for them from that place of mercy, whether you ever hear their story or not.

The Role of Witness

In your Law it is written that the testimony of two people is true. - John 8:17

The intercessor acts as a witness in a prayer session. Jesus told the Pharisees that He and the Father were the two witnesses that proved His testimony true.[63] A single witness might lie, but agreement between two witnesses established the truth.[64] The recipient can have confidence in the truth because the intercessor and God act as the two witnesses.

This takes a lot of pressure off of the intercessor. The witness affirms the truth that comes from God but is not responsible for coming up with the truth on his own. The source of truth is the Spirit and the intercessor provides confirmation.

"What do you think I should do?" asked Joan. She had just outlined a mind boggling problem that put her parents and siblings at enmity with her and each other. It was no wonder that she should seek godly advice.

"What has God told you to do?" I asked in response. I was certainly ready to take the matter back to prayer if she had not already gotten a message from Him.

As Joan shared what she thought God was telling her I nodded in agreement. The solution was brilliant, loving, and gentle. I acted as a witness for God and confirmed that this message was true and consistent with His nature. Honestly, God's way was far superior to anything I could have offered.

Sometimes the witness is called to give testimony for the recipient. If the voice he hears brings accusation and condemnation it is important to stick up for him and expose the lie of the devil. Similarly, if the message he hears is in opposition to God's revealed word then it is a stronghold and must be challenged. Sticking up for the recipient helps him discern and focus on the word of God.

There is also a role for the witness in holding the territory by attesting to the fact that a spiritual transaction has happened. The devil wants to steal or destroy[65] the healing work of God, but the witness stands against him. We give testimony to the event and act as eye witness to the change.

Mark and I prayed together one afternoon because a spirit of fear oppressed him. God revealed that he suffered from "fear of man," which is an obsession about meeting the expectations of others. We took authority over that spirit and commanded it to leave in the name of Jesus. Mark was amazed at the immediate sense of peace that replaced the fear.

Several weeks later I asked Mark how he was doing. He shared about a few current struggles that had caused him to relapse into "fear of man" thoughts and actions.

"Wait a minute!" I inserted. "We kicked that spirit of fear out last time. You said it was not welcome and we sent him packing. I was there. Remember how you were set free?"

Mark immediately recalled the previous victory and stood his ground against that spirit. My witness emboldened him to walk according to his new nature, rather than to revert back to his old ways.

Laying on Hands

Jesus blessed the children by laying His hands on them and praying for them.[66] He also laid hands on people to heal them.[67] The apostles laid hands on many to heal and to confer the gifts of the Spirit on believers.[68] Nevertheless, this is not to be treated as some ritualistic magic or practice as Simon the Magician did.[69] Jesus gave the disciples authority to use this method, and, by extension, has given all believers the same authority.[70]

I believe Jesus modeled this method in His healing ministry because it ties the spiritual, emotional and physical realms together. The Spirit is transferred from one person to another through this symbolic act. The physical realm is activated by the sense of touch. The emotional realm is involved by the thoughts and feelings that arise during the process. Complete healing brings wholeness to the person in body, soul and spirit.

Jesus touched the eyes of the blind man, the tongue of the mute man, and the ears of the deaf man. Consider the benefit of placing your hands directly on the place that needs to be healed. Often a sense of warmth, tingling, or other manifestation will accompany the transfer of the Spirit and power.

There are sexual and cultural considerations regarding appropriate touching. The intercessor should not touch another person in a way that might be misunderstood as intimacy or undue familiarity. Instead, ask the recipient to lay his or her hand on the place that needs to be healed and connect to that point by laying your hand over theirs or on the elbow or shoulder.

Cultural sensitivity comes from understanding the people group to whom you are ministering. For instance, I often place my hands on the head of a person while giving them a blessing. While this is a sign of great honor in some cultures, it is extremely demeaning in others. Be sensitive to the recipient's frame of reference.

Anointing Oil

There are many biblical examples of anointing oil used for crowning a king, honoring a guest, conferring a blessing, inviting healing, and as a sign of the Holy Spirit. I like to use anointing oil in prayer appointments because of its power to draw the spiritual, emotional and physical realms together.

I always ask a person for permission to anoint them with oil. I want to be sensitive to any potential allergic reactions or emotional aversions. Most people gladly welcome the chance to receive prayer as described in James 5:14. We use an oil that has frankincense and myrrh in it, available through many Christian supply sources. The aroma adds to the setting, activates the sense of smell and can trigger emotional connections.

There are several ways to use anointing oil, but my preferred method is to put a dab of oil on my forefinger and use it to mark a cross on the person's forehead. While doing so I make this proclamation:

"Julie, I anoint you in the name of the Father, and the Son, and the Holy Spirit."

For healing prayer, I may anoint the person at the place of pain. For instance, anointing the wrist or elbows for arthritic pain, the jaw for TMJ, or the neck for stress or back pain.

For a blessing prayer, especially for a person's calling or life purpose, I anoint his or her hands and ask God to bless the work of their hands.[71] For a commissioning for evangelism or blessing an upcoming mission trip I anoint a person's feet.[72]

Spiritual Warfare

The reason the Son of God appeared was to destroy the works of the devil. - 1 John 3:8b

All believers are given power and authority from Jesus to do His will. As it states in the verse above, He *appeared to destroy the works of the devil.* When we act in agreement with His purpose we are endowed with His power and authority to complete it.

As stated in Chapter Five, the devil is the ultimate legalist. He uses the law to accuse and condemn. The battle in the spiritual realm is all about laws and rules, rights and responsibilities. Sin transfers authority to the devil, and forgiveness takes it away from him.

What is done on earth, in the physical realm, has a direct effect on the rulers and principalities in the spiritual realm.[73] It is wise to consider the spiritual transactions that remove the legal ground from the enemy and restore relationship with the Father. That is why it is important to operate under the leadership of the Holy Spirit and the authority of Christ.

I normally ask a recipient to confess his sin aloud and ask for forgiveness as I listen. Jesus said that every charge may be established by the evidence of two or three witnesses.[74] My role is to act as a witness to the spiritual transaction in the physical realm while God is witness in the spiritual realm. Then I am able to confidently proclaim that the transaction is complete and irrefutable, thereby removing legal ground from the devil.

Dealing with evil spirits and demons is an important part of healing prayer today. The western worldview underestimates the influence of these unclean spirits, and perhaps their power is greater in the West because they are undetected.

Some churches treat demons as archaic, inconsequential, or relegated to third world countries. The entertainment industry and media outlets have sensationalized the demonic and misled many people. Unfortunately, there are some self-proclaimed demon fighters that also sensationalize spiritual warfare in a way that creates fear, which is fuel for the devil.

For these reasons I use various terms in spiritual warfare, depending on the audience. The term "demon possessed" has the connotation that the unclean spirit operates from inside the person. The term "demonic influence" can mean the same, but has the connotation of the unclean spirit working from outside of the person. The term "stronghold" can mean the same, but has the connotation of a thought pattern rather than an unclean spirit. Finally, the term "temptation" can refer to an almost overwhelming power, but replaces the concept of a demon with a more generic evil force. Any or all of these terms refer to the schemes of the devil trying to kill, steal, and destroy the works of God.

When engaged in spiritual warfare, know your authority. Work only within your authority by doing what you hear the Father telling you to do through the Spirit.[75] Understand your orders and stand firm.[76]

> *... But the people who know their God shall stand firm and take action. - Daniel 11:32*

Chapter Ten:
Prayer Strategies

"Lord, teach us to pray, as John taught his disciples." -
Luke 11:1

The disciples asked Jesus to teach them to pray. They recognized the power and authority with which He prayed and wished to pray like that. What He taught them was not an incantation, not a formula, and not a procedure. He taught them how to have a prayer strategy. It was a three year lesson that culminated with the promise *"My Father will give you whatever you ask in My name."*[77]

A prayer strategy is the way in which we pray for a given situation. It takes into consideration our motive, attitude and specific request. A confident prayer comes by knowing the will of God and agreeing with it, because when we ask *"in His name"* our prayers are powerful. They lead to transformation in us and in others, they please God, and they move heaven.

How do you know the heart of God in a matter? It requires prayer of preparation. **I ask God what I need to know to intercede properly.** *I consider how God feels about the person and the situation so I can feel the same way. I love from my heart to overcome judgment. I listen to the Spirit rather than rely on my discernment. I surrender my reputation, rights, and responsibilities. One of the hardest lessons to learn comes from our stubborn refusal to refrain from interfering in other people's lives. It takes a long time to realize the danger of being an amateur providence, that is, interfering with God's plan for others. You see someone suffering and say, "He will not suffer, and I will make sure that he doesn't." You put your hand right in front of God's permissive will to stop it, and then God says, "What is that to you?" Is there stagnation in your spiritual life? Don't allow it to continue, but get into God's presence and find out the* *reason for it. You will possibly find it is because you have been interfering in the life of another—proposing things you had no right to propose, or advising when you had no right to advise. When you do have to give advice to another person, God will advise through you with the direct understanding of His Spirit. Your part is to* **maintain the right relationship with God** *so that His discernment can come through you continually for the purpose of blessing someone else.*[78]

The heart of an intercessor maintains right relationship with God, as stated in this devotional from Oswald Chambers. It is a great privilege to share in the work of God as He reconciles the world to Himself through Christ, but it requires careful balance between humbleness and boldness. We must humbly follow God's leading while we boldly engage in meaningful participation with His plan. Humility comes from worship, and confidence comes from knowledge of the truth.

The ideas and information in this chapter are based on our experience and the experience of others. We have observed patterns and signals in our prayer appointments and share them to build your confidence. Use them to confirm what God reveals, but do not rely on them in lieu of hearing from Him.

The religious leaders of Israel misunderstood the prophecies about Messiah because they tried to use them predictively. The apostles filled the New Testament with proof that Jesus of Nazareth was the Messiah by using those same prophecies as confirmation. Applying the prophetic word after the fact was a witness to truth that could not have been imagined before the fact.

If you have had a surprise birthday party thrown for you, you have experienced an example of this concept. At the moment when everyone shouts "Happy Birthday" you are truly surprised. When the shock subsides you recall a bunch of minor details that "prophesied" the celebration. You could not have combined those details to draw a conclusion about the party before the fact. After the fact you wonder how it could have remained hidden. All the details confirm what you have come to know.

These prayer strategies are not predictive because that could lead to judgment, and even a trace of judgment in your heart will disqualify you from interceding in that matter. Rather, use these strategies to confirm the truth after it has been revealed. It may give you a direction to go in prayer, and will increase your boldness as a witness.

Addiction

"Addictive behavior is not the *problem*," says Dr. Ed Smith of Theophostic Prayer Ministry. "It is someone's *solution* to his problem." He goes on to teach that when a well-meaning helper tries to take away the recipient's solution, it does nothing to solve the problem. Either the addict reverts back to his solution when his will power fails or he takes on a substitute. Exchanging one addiction for another is not freedom, even if the new behavior is socially acceptable or considered healthy.

A prayer strategy for addiction begins with interrogating the behavior. Ask about the triggers, or circumstances, that lead to the addictive response. Inquire about the emotional response to that trigger, and use both the emotion and behavior to identify the underlying belief. The false belief is often the source of the problem. Take it captive and make it obedient to Christ.[79]

Addictions create an appetite that they promise to fill, but like any lust the appetite is a bottomless pit. Addictive behavior is not a true remedy for the problem, but masks the pain of conflict for a period of time.

Alcohol and drugs are chemicals used to numb pain and quiet fear. The problem of *pain* or *fear* may originate in any of the realms, and over time will manifest in all three.

A prayer strategy for *pain* is to identify its source and ask Jesus to heal it. Pain that originates in the physical realm, from an accident or disease for instance, needs physical healing. Pain that originates in the emotional realm often requires forgiveness and being forgiven, and then the Holy Spirit can bring comfort to that place. Pain that originates in the spiritual realm requires reconciliation, and may involve spiritual warfare.

A prayer strategy for *fear* is to identify its source through listening prayer. When the recipient is willing to confess the fear it opens the door for God to calm it and replace the fear with His peace. Fear can arise from any of the realms, but is often seated in the emotional realm.

Addiction to drugs and alcohol causes a chemical imbalance in the body. I have seen God heal that imbalance immediately while simultaneously healing the source of the problem in the emotional realm. I have also seen God heal a chemical imbalance over time, as the toxins and active agents are filtered from the body through normal processes.

Drug and alcohol addictions are often the result of generational curses. A child or young adult rarely considers the use of poison as a good solution to their problem unless it has been modeled by others in their life. The devil uses the sinful choices of one's family of origin as legal ground to infect people when they are most vulnerable. Breaking these generational curses is often a part of a prayer strategy for overcoming chemical addiction.

Fantasy addictions are a means of mental escape and include pornography, video gaming, romance novels, and media. The need for escape often originates in the emotional realm, so the prayer strategy will include inner healing.

Catherine Thorpe, a licensed mental health practitioner and author of *The Healing Timeline*[80] said that she has never encountered a man addicted to pornography that did not have a lonely eleven year old boy inside. The loneliness may come from rejection, abandonment, or the result of poor self-assessment. Latch-key kids, introverts, loners, and boys that are bullied are particularly susceptible.

A spirit of *porneo* is a demon that exercises authority over someone by claiming legal ground because of sexual sin. It is often a sin committed by the person affected, but it can also be the result of sexual sin committed against that person. For instance, children that have been sexually abused are subject to this unclean spirit through no fault of their own. Sexual abuse may include any loss of innocence at the hands of another.

There are many sexual sins that open the door to temptations and oppression, such as promiscuity, adultery, fornication, rape, or any sexual perversion. People with sins of this type often confuse sex with love, and try to gain acceptance through physical intimacy. These are some of the markers that point to problems related to sexual issues.

Whenever one person overrides the free will of another it is abuse. The abused person is manipulated into loss of control and may respond by ceding all future control (victimization) or by becoming a control freak. Pornography lends itself to the second response because the one fantasizing maintains absolute control over each scenario.

Although pornography generally originates in the emotional or spiritual realms, it soon has an effect in the physical realm as well. Like a baby's pacifier, the fantasy establishes mental associations and releases endorphins that bring temporary calm to the body. The recipient must regain control over this reflex, either naturally or supernaturally, to be free from the snare. A prayer strategy is to cover the sexual sins with forgiveness, evict the spirit of *porneo,* and pray for recovered innocence.

Romance novels and romantic comedy movies are more often the snare for women in similar situations. She can lose herself in the idea of "perfect love," and that mental escape releases endorphins and brings a temporary feeling of calm. A prayer strategy includes a request for healing her loneliness and that she will discover and accept her true identity.

Gamers usually became addicted at a young age. Some of them, as latch-key kids, played video games out of boredom or loneliness. Others played them to find acceptance in a virtual gaming community that they were not getting in real life. Still others looked for purpose or value and turned to fantasy to be good at something. A prayer strategy may key in on acceptance, purpose, challenge, or value. God may bring the recipient back to the time when he chose gaming as a coping strategy so a "new" decision can be made. In some cases spiritual warfare is warranted because the nature of many video games is idolatrous and occultic.

Media addiction is characterized by a constant flood of information, the sheer volume of which has a numbing effect on the mind. Activities can include watching movies or television, being dependent on noise from the radio, or paying constant attention to social media. Media addiction is a way of hiding and a prayer strategy is to uncover the thing that causes fear, pain, or another intrusion from which the person is hiding.

Behavioral addictions tend to be used as coping strategies for false beliefs and broken identities. The prayer strategy is to uncover the root issue that drives the behavior, and then allow God to minister to that place.

Retail therapy, the addiction of buying unneeded things, is generally rooted in low self-esteem. The "gifting" is perceived as a personal reward, though the feeling of worth is fleeting. The prayer strategy may be inner healing to overcome the sense of low self-worth.

Hoarding, or the accumulation of stuff, is generally rooted in a poverty mentality. This mindset believes there is never enough. It can also accompany an orphan mentality, which is the belief that one must provide for and protect oneself. A prayer strategy is to reveal God as the source of all good things.

Hiding, which includes isolation and withdrawal, often arises from feelings of guilt and shame. The prayer strategy may include breaking off word curses, particularly if the person got the message that he would never amount to anything or never measure up. Unconfessed sin can also lead to hiding strategies, and these sins can come to light through the conviction of the Holy Spirit.

A related addiction is "hiding things" which is the behavior of keeping items or information from others in an unhealthy way. This may be due to shame, embarrassment, or a poverty mentality. Pray that the truth be revealed to replace the belief that underlies those emotions.

Obsessions are forms of idolatry because the thing that holds top position in the mind becomes an object of worship. The mind places objects of fear in the highest priority and often the obsession is rooted in some fear. Physical and mental obsessions can be healed as the prayer recipient discovers the truth about his identity and allows God to guard against any perceived danger.

Trauma

"Trauma is an emotional response to a terrible event like an accident, rape or natural disaster. Immediately after the event, shock and denial are typical. Longer term reactions include unpredictable emotions, flashbacks, strained relationships and even physical symptoms like headaches or nausea," explains the American Psychological Association in the APA Help Center.[81]

Any trauma can be an opportunity for the devil to gain legal ground through sin and temptation. The mind of a person that suffers a trauma is compelled to resolve, or assign meaning, to the event, its beliefs and emotions. The devil offers to help resolve the conflict in exchange for authority.

The most common traps are bitterness, unforgiveness, confusion and victimization.

A prayer strategy for trauma may include revisiting the scene of the trauma in a memory or vision. Pray that God will bring resolution to the mental conflict, and heal the memory with His *shalom*.

Unforgiveness is a typical response to trauma. The offense of the trauma represents an unpaid debt to the one who was traumatized. The mind considers it unreasonable to release the debt without getting something of value in return, but that puts the victim in a perpetual position as debt collector. The prayer strategy is for the recipient to identify the offense (take an account), and choose to release it.

Bitterness is a replacement emotion. The mind attempts to assign an appropriate emotion to the event, but since it is unresolved this is impossible. Anger, disappointment, fear, sadness, and many other feelings might be expressed, but none seem to fit the situation just right. So the soul assigns bitterness as a "temporary" catch-all emotion. Unfortunately, this pending emotion can persist for many years.

A prayer strategy for overcoming bitterness recognizes this emotion and helps the recipient choose to release it. It will be replaced with an appropriate emotion. While an emotion is neither good nor bad, there are appropriate emotions. If a person feels the same way about an event as God feels about it, that is an appropriate emotion.

For example, Robert was bitter because his neighbor, a trusted family friend, had sexually abused him when he was young. As we prayed, God brought him to a memory of one episode, so I asked God to reveal truth to Robert in the midst of that memory. Robert saw Jesus in that memory picture, and knew He was very sad. I assured Robert that sadness was an appropriate emotion for him as well. This resolved the bitterness and gave Robert room to forgive his neighbor, and he was healed from the trauma immediately.

When a child is traumatized, he is unable to come up with an explanation for the event and confusion becomes his primary emotional response. The lie of the devil twists the confusion in the circumstance (I do not understand) into a state of confusion (I cannot understand). A traumatized person with a persistent state of confusion gives up trying to make sense of anything. The prayer strategy is for him to receive a sound mind[82] and full restoration of his personhood.

Trauma can also give a person the false identity of "victim." While it is true that in the traumatic event the person was a victim, it is not true that this has become his identity. We refer to this as a "victim-mentality" when it is the way he begins to self-identify. The victim needs to be rescued from this false identity, otherwise he will seek out another abuser or controller and the cycle repeats.

A prayer strategy against a victim-mentality includes asking God to reveal the recipient's true identity. A victim may believe he only has value in what he provides to the abuser, but God will reveal that he was created on purpose and has always been valuable.[83]

Anxiety

> *Do not be anxious about anything, but in everything by prayer and supplication with thanksgiving let your requests be made known to God. And the peace of God, which surpasses all understanding, will guard your hearts and your minds in Christ Jesus. - Philippians 4:6-7*

Anxiety is a habit. It is a bad habit that can be hard to break, but it is just a habit. Anxiousness starts when you perceive a threat and your brain tries to work out a solution. As stated earlier, fear holds the top position in the mind until it is resolved. The mind works tirelessly to resolve it so new and less threatening thoughts can be entertained. Additionally, there is a pleasure center in your brain that rewards you every time you come up with a solution to a problem. It is the reason you like discovering new things.

The problem becomes severe when there is no solution to the threat. The lazy brain gives up and the person moves toward withdrawal, passivity and depression. The active brain keeps searching for a solution, expending effort on "what-if" scenarios but never being rewarded with an answer. Creative people can be the most susceptible to this issue. The symptoms of anxiousness escalate from perceiving a threat to worry, from worry to anxiety, and from anxiety to panic.

The prayer strategy begins with finding the source of fear that drives the behavior so it can be released to God. The recipient that places his trust in himself must confess that as idolatry and receive forgiveness. Then repentance can come in the form of offering thanksgiving and allowing God to protect his heart with peace.

Like other addictions, anxiety and chronic fear produce a chemical response in the body that must be healed. For example, excess adrenalin creates problems in the physical realm such as elevated blood pressure, rapid breathing, and increased heart rate. The body adapts to this chemical imbalance over time and must be "reset" to the divine design. Pray for physical healing once the root of anxiety has been removed.

Physical Healing

The following section was compiled from experience and observation about the physical manifestation of emotional and spiritual conflict. It is not intended to be a checklist for judgment, nor a grid for diagnoses. After all, even a trace of judgment in your heart toward a person disqualifies you from interceding in that matter. Use it only as a guideline to confirm what the Spirit has revealed through prayer.[84]

>Arthritis- bitterness, unforgiveness, fear, anger.

>Asthma- fear, abuse, rejection, self-loathing, unforgiveness.

>Autoimmune disorders- self-loathing, self-rejection, betrayal, fear, hopelessness.

Bone problems - fear of man, pretense.

Cancer- bitterness, unforgiveness, anger, low self-esteem.

Diabetes- rejection issues, fear, low self-esteem.

Digestive issues- stress, unresolved conflict, anger, rejection.

Headache- fear, stress, relationship conflict, anger.

Heart conditions- fear, stress, anger, unforgiveness.

Kidney, bladder, digestive problems- fear, bitterness.

Liver, gall bladder- anger, judgmental, anxiety, bitterness.

Obesity- low self-esteem, anger, unforgiveness, stress.

Prostate- rejection, low self-esteem.

Reproductive- self-loathing, stress, anxiety, anger.

Respiratory- grief, sorrow, abandonment.

Stomach, spleen- worry, fear, depression.

Type A personality- fear of man, rejection, word curse.

Victimization- fear, failure to thrive, lack of identity, generational curse, demonization.

Inner Healing

The key for inner healing is to discover and accept one's true identity. A false identity arises out of misinterpretations and bad conclusions. The prayer strategy is to identify and then interrogate the belief to make it obedient to Christ. Ask God to reveal the source of the false belief so it can be thoroughly investigated.

Many times the prayer session for inner healing goes back to interactions with parents, siblings, or others previously held as an authority. We do not explore these connections to place blame, but to discover what must be forgiven. We find the root not out of morbid curiosity, but so God can apply the truth in place of the lie.

False conclusions can be drawn in the most innocuous of circumstances. For instance, I grew up being very shy and insecure. God revealed the source and gave me truth in its place.

One day, when I was eight years old, I found one of my older sisters crying in her closet. I asked Laura what was wrong.

"I have an inferiority complex," she said with all the authority of a twelve year old.

"What's an inferiority complex?" I asked.

"It's when you think there is something wrong with you because you're not as good as anyone else," she explained.

"Why would you think that?" I wondered aloud.

"Well, Thelma (our oldest sister) is smart and I could never be as smart as her. Nancy (the next oldest) is sweet and beautiful, and everyone thinks she's an angel. I could never be as sweet or nice as her. That leaves me (next in age), and I just don't measure up," she explained through her tears.

I had no idea how to comfort her so I went off to play. Then I began thinking about what she had said.

"Thelma is smarter than me, too. Nancy is sweeter and nicer than I could ever be, too. Cliff (my older brother) is way stronger than me. And Laura has a better inferiority complex than me. I must have one, too," I reasoned.

I was plagued by this inferiority complex well into adulthood. My coping strategies (humor, sarcasm, withdrawal, and introversion) were so advanced that acquaintances and casual friends did not suspect I was shy and insecure.

When God brought it to my attention through prayer I could quickly see how the simple faith of my eight year old self accepted this identity by association with an older sister whom I loved and respected. I forgave my sister for inadvertently leading me astray, and I confessed the sin of

144

believing the lie about my identity. God forgave the offenses and immediately began revealing my identity in Christ - my true identity.

Rejection & Abandonment

God is a Triune Godhead and the body of Christ is made up of many members. We are designed to operate in community and to be *cut off* is a consequence of sin.[85] Rejection and abandonment are punishments that cut off a person.

Rejection is personal because it conveys that you are not chosen. The person who experiences rejection often believes he is unlovable or that he has done something unforgivable. The prayer strategy is to discover where this conclusion was drawn so God can reveal truth in its place.

A baby from an unwanted pregnancy experiences rejection before birth. A child that is treated as an inconvenience experiences rejection early in life. A school aged child that does not fit in experiences rejection from his classmates. The dynamics of middle school and high school are rife with rejection. Adulthood is not exempt from it either, though the "rejection mindset" has usually been accepted before then.

The prayer strategy may include a visit to the time or setting in which the recipient came to believe he was rejected. Then God can reveal the truth about eternal relationship with Him in its place.

For example, Nick had severe rejection issues when he came for prayer. He was raised by a single mom and life was a struggle. He felt the sting of rejection when he went to school and got a glimpse of how other students lived. At six years old he realized how lonely he was and came to believe he must be an unlovable bother.

We asked God to reveal truth to him in that memory. Nick recalled the moment when his six-year-old mind decided he was unlovable. He suddenly felt the unmistakable presence of God. The feeling convinced him that God loved him

"Remind me again, when were you saved?" I asked him.

"At nineteen. It was my freshman year of college and I went to an InterVarsity retreat," he answered.

"Amazing!" I observed. "God loved you thirteen years before you accepted Him!"

Where rejection conveys "you are not chosen," abandonment implies "I choose me, and there is no room for you." Both actions sever relationship and cause pain, so the prayer strategies are similar. Death, divorce, and deployment are common sources of abandonment.

The person who experiences abandonment often believes he is unlovable, unworthy, or has something fundamentally wrong with him. The prayer strategy begins with the recipient forgiving those that are responsible for the abandonment. Once that has been released there is opportunity for God to provide the nurture and acceptance that is so necessary for maturity.

People that have been adopted are not exempt from rejection and abandonment. The devil sows seeds of discord and takes legal ground because of sin in the biological family of origin. The prayer strategy may include dealing with generational curses, word curses, and early life influences. Forgiving those that rejected and abandoned is different than rationalizing or justifying it. The offense must be released before true acceptance can be experienced.

Betrayal

Betray means to deliver or expose someone to the power of an enemy by treachery or disloyalty. It is worse than violence or injustice. It is a form of abuse that disturbs the very core of one's identity, and it is the basis for all mistrust. Unresolved betrayal leads to pessimism, suspicion and isolation. It causes selfishness, just as it is caused by selfishness.

Betrayal happens when pressure forces a betrayer to decide for self over love. From narcissist (slightest provocation) to saint-like (under duress), when push comes to shove, the betrayer says: "I will sacrifice you on my behalf." Whatever he is trying to gain or protect becomes the standard by which he measures the other person. Judas valued the personhood of Jesus at thirty pieces of silver. Often the trade is made for something less tangible than silver, such as position, reputation, or opportunity.

The human response to being betrayed may be internal, where the victim moves toward self-protection by putting up facades, defensive walls to thwart future attacks, or isolation. He may become unwilling or unable to trust, and cannot help but become distrustful of God.

The response may be external, where the victim lashes out in anger and aggressiveness in a first-strike strategy. He may harbor bitterness that affects all relationships. He may plan or dream of retaliation, and blame God for allowing the injustice.

The prayer strategy requires that the recipient forgive his betrayer and receive his worth from God rather than what was exchanged in the betrayal.

Check for remaining symptoms of betrayal: distrust of God, anger, aloofness, bitterness, pessimistic or cynical outlook. Pray that the recipient be restored so he is no longer afraid to be vulnerable in relationships, and able to fulfill his destiny.

Chapter Eleven:
You are My Praise

Heal me, O LORD, and I shall be healed; save me, and I shall be saved, for You are my praise. - Jeremiah 17:14

How are you doing?

The healed person honestly answers: "I am happy to be me and I am willing to live forever with God, just as I am."

This expresses reconciliation with God. It depicts harmony with God by the Spirit-to-spirit communication link, unity with Him through agreement of my spirit and soul, and faith that He will not allow my body to interrupt our relationship. This reconciled condition leads to joy and praise.

The verse above can be paraphrased with an injection of faith as: "Be healing (doctoring) me, O LORD, and I am as good as healed. Be saving (reconciling) me, and I am as good as reconciled." Since healing and saving are progressive, fresh joy and praise are continuous! I cannot help but smile when I witness a healing - it never gets old.

We instruct a person that has been healed to share the good news with someone that day. Confession builds faith. As he tells about what happened it builds praise, and as he verbalizes the truth he feels the emotions of God. Sharing the truth helps makes it come alive in the spiritual, emotional and physical realms.

We also ask what he can do to mark the occasion. Some make journal entries to capture the details of the event, much like a Book of Remembrance.[86] Others choose a physical sign, such as a rock or memorial like Samuel did at Ebenezer.[87] Still others perform an act of repentance as taught by John the Baptist.[88] The list goes on, but the exciting thing is how the Holy Spirit guides this process. When we ask Him if there is something the recipient should do in response to the healing an idea comes to the person's mind almost immediately. In every case the action has been perfectly suited to the person and his healing.

Redeemed Story

God heals retroactively! This is an exciting truth because it means God's redeeming power in the present has an altering effect on the past. It is a miracle that God is able to give us a *new* history!

Melissa came for prayer because of rejection she felt her whole life. She was placed in an orphanage as an infant by her birth mother. She was adopted by a poor family where she was treated as an expense and bother. She was sexually abused and emotionally tormented until she ran away from home. She was legally emancipated at age sixteen. Her adult life was filled with broken relationships and disappointments. She could not recall a single act of kindness or acceptance by another human being in her thirty-seven years.

God healed Melissa by giving her a new identity. He revealed Himself to her in a way that proved His love for her. She saw how He had been with her throughout her hard life, never leaving her side. She was a new creation.

After she was healed God showed her how people had accepted and loved her as a child. In her pain she had rebuffed some great acts of kindness. Slowly she rebuilt her history in the light of God's truth - that she was loved. God gave her a new history by redeeming the events and conclusions of her whole life. She recounted many acts of kindness and acceptance and began to give God the praise.

In another example, Edward came to a prayer workshop filled with guilt. He was preoccupied with the disclosure comments used at the beginning of the class. The shame he felt was so bad he was not willing to talk about the trauma. He could not imagine the pain he would experience if word got out about what he had been through.

I prayed with Edward privately and witnessed an incredible miracle. God accepted his request for forgiveness, covered his guilt, and comforted him from the shame. He was a new creation!

At the end of the workshop we asked for volunteers to share a testimony. Edward stood and shared about the amazing healing God had given him. I rejoiced because his testimony of forgiveness was powerful, and the public confession proved he was completely free from the guilt and shame.

When a story is a container for pain, it wants to be hidden. When a story is filled with God's goodness it is an opportunity for praise, even loud and public praise!

Practice your testimony. Rehearse the goodness of God so you can effectively share about His character. You will find that your story becomes more about God and less about you as you express your healing. Your testimony is a way to share love and comfort with your audience and it may encourage them toward a deeper relationship with God.

A Suitable Thank Offering

> *Then Noah built an altar to the LORD and took some of every clean animal and some of every clean bird and offered burnt offerings on the altar.* - *Genesis 8:20*

Noah thanked God with a burnt offering, and when the LORD smelled the pleasing aroma He promised never to curse the ground or strike down every living creature again. The thank offering was a suitable response of praise to God for salvation.

It is a privilege to act as witness to the spiritual transaction by which God reconciles man to Himself through Christ.[89] One of the follow up questions we have learned to ask is: "Has God asked you to do anything, or does anything come to your heart, that is an appropriate response to this healing?"

We never presume to know what action is called for because God has a way of making this step very personal. One woman knew immediately that she needed to burn love letters from an old boyfriend. A man immediately knew he needed to write a letter to the one he had forgiven. Another woman was prompted to destroy jewelry that had been used in pagan rituals, and another man was prompted to purge his home of artwork that was associated with idolatry.

Jacob wrestled with God one night to receive the blessing that changed his name to Israel and renewed the Abrahamic covenant. His response was to set up a pillar and pour out a drink offering.[90] It was a suitable response to the LORD.

"What are you filling yourself up with that does not satisfy, in place of the living water of Jesus?" asked one of the women at a prayer retreat a few years ago.

Immediately my wife was convicted by the Holy Spirit that Diet Coke was something she drank as a little pick-me-up or personal reward. She admitted that it was a temporary fix at best. Then she repented of her attitude and asked God to forgive her for not accepting His living water that truly satisfies. Prompted by the Spirit, she opened a can and poured it out before the Lord as a drink offering. As she watched it flow down the drain she felt the "coke urge" drain out of her. She breathed a great sigh of relief as she felt God fill her with living water.

Our ministry is a publicly supported non-profit organization that allows us to pray with people without charge because we are completely funded by donations. Some contribute to our ministry to support the work of God, and others make a free will offering because they benefit from a time of prayer. It is always exciting to see how God provides.

Last year we received an unexpected gift from the estate of a family friend. We felt led to host a "Thank Offering Party" in celebration. This was the second such party we have held, and it was so much fun that we hope to be prompted to do it again. It was a time of sharing, celebrating, praising, and proclaiming God's goodness.

The patterns of the feasts of the Lord served as our guide:

There must be family and friends invited from all over to join us in the celebration.

There must be food in generous proportions to be shared by all.

There must be worship music, loud noise, clapping, and movement offered to the Lord in praise.

There must be testimony as we recount the blessings of the Lord and tell of His goodness.

Finally, there must be rejoicing because the Kingdom of God is here.

I bless you to experience the fullness of joy in the Lord, and to follow His prompting to make a suitable thank offering to Him.

Now to Him who is able to do far more abundantly than all that we ask or think, according to the power at work within us, to Him be glory in the church and in Christ Jesus throughout all generations, forever and ever. Amen.
- Ephesians 3:20-21

Resources

About the Author

Calvin Tadema is the founder of Master's Mind Ministry. He and his wife, Julie, are a ministry team based near Vancouver, Washington. Their prayer ministry is built on individual prayer appointments for healing in the spiritual, emotional and physical realms. They teach about listening prayer, reconciliation, and deeper relationship with God. They also conduct workshops and seminars to equip others in healing prayer.

Other Titles

These books are also available through Two Worlds Press (www.twoworldsmedia.com):

Marriage Rx: Prescription for a radical marriage

By Dan & Jody Mayhew, Calvin & Julie Tadema - 2013.

Marriage Rx is a code name that came as a response to the news that yet another Christian marriage was headed for divorce. We agreed that the schemes of the enemy included the destruction of marriages, derailing those that have been called to serve, and taking out those that should be spiritual leaders. What was God's prescription for this epidemic?

We went away to a quiet place to pray and seek His face. Out of that prayer time came a picture of God's intentions for marriage. This book is not a new list of actions and behaviors to help husbands and wives get along better, it is a description of the character and identity of God reflected through married Christians living as examples of His nature. *Marriage Rx* is about your marriage - all of our marriages - but more than that, it is about His marriage: Christ and His church.

The Ancient Deceptions: Uncover the oldest tricks in The Book

By Jody Mayhew and Julie Tadema - 2014.

Lies ... When we believe them, they may as well be true. When we discover the truth, deception loses its power.

The Ancient Deceptions helps you uncover the lies that have been around since the first humans believed them and shows you how to keep from falling for the oldest tricks in The Book.

Speaking and Teaching

Calvin and Julie Tadema regularly teach workshops, classes, seminars and retreats near their home in the Pacific Northwest and by invitation to churches and groups nationally and internationally.

Go to www.mastersmindministry.org for free support materials, including articles, newsletters, worksheets, audio and video presentations, and upcoming training classes. Use this site to inquire about their availability to speak or teach in your community.

Master's Mind Ministry

21811 NE 164th St

Brush Prairie, WA 98606

Endnotes

[1] Oswald Chambers, *My Utmost for His Highest* (Discovery House, Grand Rapids, MI, 1935, 1963) December 15

[2] An Ebenezer refers to the rock Samuel set up as a testimony to God's faithfulness. 1 Samuel 7:12

[3] Proverbs 14:1

[4] Luke 9:1

[5] Ephesians 4:13

[6] "Since ancient times, leprosy has been regarded by the community as a contagious, mutilating and incurable disease." - World Health Organization, *Leprosy: the disease*

[7] John 17:24

[8] 2 Corinthians 3:17-18

[9] Genesis 3:16-19

[10] John 16:8

[11] Philippians 4:7

[12] James 2:19

[13] Luke 9:1

[14] Luke 4:18

[15] Matthew 14:16; Mark 6:37; Luke 9:13

[16] John 21:17

[17] Luke 10:9

[18] Matthew 7:7

[19] Acts 9:3-7

[20] Exodus 7:3-5

[21] 2 Kings 6:17

[22] Ephesians 1:20

[23] Ephesians 6:12

[24] Leviticus 24:16

[25] Genesis 3:14, 17

[26] Romans 12:14

[27] Genesis 8:21

[28] Romans 12:14

[29] Revelation 12:10

[30] Romans 8:28

31 Philippians 4:8
32 2 Corinthians 5:17
33 Ezekiel 36:26
34 Romans 8:17, 20
35 1 Corinthians 15:42-44
36 1 Peter 2:20
37 2 Kings 20
38 John 6:2
39 Matthew 15:30-31
40 Luke 24:49
41 Luke 6:6-10
42 Luke 5:17-24
43 John 11:37-44
44 John 5:14
45 Nehemiah 9:21
46 Job 14:5
47 1 John 1:9
48 Exodus 20:8
49 Isaiah 56:6-7
50 Matthew 9:6
51 Job 2:9
52 Mark 9:23
53 Hebrews 4:11
54 John 8:44
55 Revelation 12:10
56 Genesis 1:26-27
57 Matthew 16:33
58 The "church of the heart" refers to the body of Christ made up of all believers, irrespective of their geographic limitations, doctrinal differences, traditions and cultures.
59 Genesis 11:6
60 Crabb and Allendar, *Encouragement: The Key to Caring* (Grand Rapids, Zondervan, 1984), p. 92
61 *Ibid.*
62 Matthew 19:22
63 John 8:18
64 Deuteronomy 17:6; Deuteronomy 19:15
65 John 10:10
66 Matthew 19:13, 15

[67] Mark 6:5

[68] Acts 8:17; 1 Timothy 4:14

[69] Acts 8:18-23

[70] Mark 16:18

[71] Psalm 90:16-17

[72] Romans 10:15

[73] Matthew 16:19

[74] Matthew 18:16

[75] John 8:28

[76] Daniel 11:32

[77] John 16:23

[78] Oswald Chambers, *My Utmost for His Highest* (Discovery House, Grand Rapids, MI, 1935, 1963) November 15

[79] 2 Corinthians 10:5

[80] Catherine Thorpe, *The Healing Timeline* (Timeline Press, LLC, 2008).

[81] http://apa.org/topics/trauma/index.aspx

[82] 2 Timothy 1:7

[83] Ephesians 2:10

[84] For an extensive knowledge base of the spiritual and emotional roots to physical problems see: Henry W. Wright, *A More Excellent Way* (Thomaston, GA, 2003).

[85] Leviticus 18:29

[86] Malachi 3:16

[87] 1 Samuel 7:12

[88] Matthew 3:8

[89] 2 Corinthians 5:19

[90] Genesis 35:14

Notes

Notes

Notes